Takes More Than Love

A memoir of racial trauma, marriage, and finding your voice

Jenna Winters

UpLit Press

I dedicate this book to my children, four of the most amazing people this world will ever know. In everything I do, you are my motivation to be better and press forward when things get hard. I love you in too many ways to count.

Chapter 1

First Comes Love

"**D**amas y caballeros, bienvenidos a Buenos Aires." Welcome to Buenos Aires. Those words were music to my ears. After spending the first five months of 2007 working while living with my parents in Omaha to save money, I had finally touched down in the city I was going to call home for the next little while. How long was the next little while? Dios sabrá. Only God knows. A wave of relief and a feeling of weightlessness overtook me.

As a Black woman, living in the United States was a constant balancing act of staying connected to my culture while making sure not to be so Black that I made white people uncomfortable. I needed to feel free to express myself for the sake of my mental health while making sure not to express myself too much and fall into the trap of being labeled sensitive, loud, or worse—angry. Being Black in the States meant being followed in stores I had no intention of ever stealing from (and that's only *if* I was acknowledged at all) and policing my speech and tone to appear educated in white spaces, but not "too white" in spaces of color.

But none of that mattered now. The U.S. was five thousand miles behind me and with a native-like fluency in Spanish, no one would guess that I called the States home. It was not uncommon for me, while abroad, to encounter countless people who tried to peg where I was from. The locals could hear that I didn't speak like them, but they always thought I was from a Spanish-speaking country.

"*Colombia?*"

"*La República Dominicana?*"

"*Ecuador?*"

"*Panamá?*"

"*No,*" I would always reply, kindly. "*Soy de los Estados Unidos.*" I'm from the United States.

"*No me digas! Pero hablas bien el español!*" No way! But you speak Spanish so well! To this day, that remains one of the best compliments that I could ever receive.

Ryan and I met within hours of my arrival to the city. Though not doing mission work myself, I was set up to live with a missionary family that my church back in the States had introduced me to. The father in the family, a tall, slender Argentine man whose dark hair was receding, was an elder at a local congregation in Buenos Aires, and he explained to me that two guys from the U.S. had just arrived the day before. They'd be in town for two months to work at the church—*la Iglesia de Dios.*

"Their names are Ryan and Wes. They go to school in Tennessee. They'll be joining us for lunch today."

"Okay," I said, trying to sound upbeat even though I wasn't particularly intrigued. Truth be told, I didn't want to be overly interested. Two years earlier, while still enrolled as a student at the University of Florida, I'd spent a semester abroad in Quito, Ecuador. It was a personally formative time, but my bond with the other U.S.-born exchange students held me back in my acquisition of Spanish and limited my chance to have an abundance of experiences that mirrored those of the local Ecuadorians. This time, I wasn't interested in bonding with others from the States—I wanted to lose myself in Argentine culture and develop friendships with *porteños* (how people from Buenos Aires refer to themselves). I did not want to make the same mistake I made the last time by insulating myself with other English speakers and keeping the world that I had just entered at arm's length.

A couple of hours after meeting my host family and starting to unpack, there was a knock at the door. As my host father opened the door, I gathered with the rest of my host family—the mother, a short, heavier-set American-born with dirty blonde hair, and their two teenage daughters whose hair they got from their dad, but light eyes they inherited from their mom—to greet our guests. In walked Ryan and Wes, two guys who were taking in their new surroundings just as much as I was. Though similar in stature, Wes, with his southern twang, hailed from East Texas, while Ryan was from North Dakota. Wes had a more muscular build, while Ryan was lean and slender. I noticed that both young men had blue eyes—Wes's were crystal-clear pools; Ryan's weren't as vibrant. Both guys had a friendly disposition about them.

My host father immediately made introductions between the guys and his family, and then them and me. "This is Jenna. She'll be living with us for a while."

I thrust my hand in Ryan's direction, then Wes's. "Hi. You can call me Jenn—Jenna's fine, too. Just not Jenny." I gave a nervous giggle. Each guy shook my hand, Wes's shake being firmer than Ryan's gentler grasp.

"Got it," Wes said and smiled.

"Where are you from, Jenn?" Ryan asked me.

"Omaha, Nebraska."

Ryan's face lit up. "Is that close to Lincoln? My sister's going to law school there."

"Nice! It's not too far. About a forty-five-minute drive. So, how long are you guys here for?"

"Two months," Wes cut in. "What about you?"

"I don't know," I said, laughing as I threw my arms up with a dramatic shrug. "I came down here on a one-way ticket and told my parents I would see them when I see them. My plan is to get certified to teach English and then live on that income."

Ryan looked amused. "That's adventurous of you," he said and laughed.

Lunch that day with Ryan, Wes, and my host family was nice. It was immediately comfortable, and I decided it wouldn't be so bad if I had friendships with people who reminded me of life back in the States. We were all around the same age—Ryan was twenty-five, I was three years younger than him, and Wes was a year younger than me. We were familiar with the same songs, watched the same TV shows, and used the same slang.

The guys told me that one of their summer projects was to make a CD of children's church songs. Though I wasn't involved in that, we ended up practicing some of the songs together after lunch. As I stood next to Ryan and Ryan next to Wes, we harmonized while singing songs I was just learning. It was a bit unsettling to sing next to people I had only just met. I was self-conscious because I didn't know the words or notes as well, but when I looked up at Wes and Ryan, I could see they were too focused on singing their best to pay attention to how I was doing. I was impressed by Ryan's vocal tone.

As our time together wound down that day and Ryan and Wes prepared to leave, one of the daughters of my host family decided it was important to memorialize this meeting. We snapped several pictures—the first of many that would come that summer. It's those first photos, though, that remain extremely special to me. I have pictures that capture the day I met my husband.

Even though I spent a majority of my time traveling around Buenos Aires teaching English, I saw a lot of Ryan and Wes since they were so connected to the family I was staying with. We spent a lot of time together—a dynamic trio. While Wes had a youthful and infectious energy to him, I gravitated more toward Ryan's temperament. He was the kind of guy who enjoyed being around people but didn't have to be the center of attention. He could often be found sitting in the background, watching the scene before him unfold. And though he often had things to say, he would quietly wait his turn, speaking when he found a natural opening in the conversation. I found him to be different than most people I was used to interacting with and attributed these qualities to him being older and more mature. Despite what I perceived to be his thoughtful maturity, there were times when he was just as playful as Wes and me.

Ryan liked to catch me off guard. One day, as we were making a routine trip to the corner store, I was gabbing about one of my new students.

"She's a flavorist! She literally develops flavors for all these different foods. Her desk has lots of—" I stopped short and looked at him, puzzled as he kept walking casually. "Did you just kick me in the butt?"

Yes. Yes, he had. In one swift motion as we walked side by side, Ryan used the leg closest to me and playfully kicked back diagonally, striking me directly on my backside. To my question, he looked over his shoulder and smirked at me as if to say "Yep, I just did that," and kept walking. I loved it. I caught up with him and we laughed our heads off as we continued to make our way to the store.

Ryan happily announced early on that summer that he grew up learning how to cook, and he often generously prepared dishes for

Wes and me. As someone who couldn't navigate her way around the kitchen very well, I stood nearby and watched in awe. He liked to cook? I couldn't believe it. Throughout my teenage years, my mom desperately tried to get me to stand next to her while she made food in order to teach me her ways and I refused every time.

As she grabbed for spices and slotted spoons, she'd often ask, "Jenna, what are you going to do when you get married and have a family?"

"I'll marry someone who knows how to cook," I'd answer every time, not knowing if that was actually a real possibility. My mom would sigh, half-exasperated, half-amused as I made a quick exit from the kitchen.

Yet here, in Buenos Aires, I was seeing for the first time a man who knew how to dice chicken, make broth from scratch, and blend spices. Usually while Ryan worked his magic, Wes and I stood close by and jammed to our favorite Spanish-language songs.

"*Tengo*," I belted out. "*Tengo la camisa ne*—ow!" I felt a sharp sting to the back of my thigh. I whipped around and found a mischievously smiling Ryan holding a dishtowel. "Ryan! You jerk!" I reached for a nearby towel and our towel-whipping war was on.

I loved being around Ryan, and it turned out that the feeling was mutual.

"Jenn, you remind me of my sister," Ryan told me one night while sitting at the dining room table in the home where he lived.

"Is that a good thing?" I asked.

"Oh yeah. I love my sister. We've always been really close. You're playful like her and go along with my randomness. Being with you feels like being with her—just really comfortable."

I smiled. "I love that. I hope I get to meet her one day."

Our connection was so strong that Ryan and I started to seek out opportunities for just the two of us to hang out—we called them "friend dates." We held hands, and he kissed my forehead after walking me to my doorstep at the end of our time together.

We were carefree and happy to be with one another; we would link arms and skip down the sidewalks of Buenos Aires. Our faces were plastered with grins that virtually forced oncoming strangers to adopt cheerful dispositions. Those are the only memories I have of skipping as an adult without a kid in sight. Saying "I love you" was commonplace for the two of us, though we never said it in the romantic sense. We just enjoyed each other as humans and had no problem expressing it.

The other people around us—other members of the church, Wes, my host family—had taken notice of our preference for one another. They were watching how we treated each other and started asking us if something more than friendship was developing. We always laughed it off, vehemently denying anything other than a platonic kinship.

During my second month in Buenos Aires, the church we attended hosted a Friends Camp a few hours outside of the city on an expansive grassy property. It had lots of open space along with cabins for sleeping and a large recreational center for socializing and eating. For those deeply rooted in their faith as well as those who were curious to know more about God, this camp was meant to bring people together for praise and worship. We chartered a Greyhound bus to drive us the three or four hours to our destination. As I made my way across town to the bus, I had it in my head that I would sit with Ryan. When I arrived, I handed off my bag to be put underneath the bus with the rest of the luggage. Excited at the prospect of us sitting together, I climbed the stairs and began to eagerly look for him.

It took a few seconds, but soon our eyes met. I smiled wide and barreled down the aisle toward him. Just as I reached his row, my smile faded as I saw that there was someone slumped down in the seat next to him. Trying to hide my disappointment, I gave him a small smile, touched his shoulder, and chose a seat a few rows back.

Friends Camp fostered a lot of new connections, but if Ryan and I caught a glimpse of one another in a crowd, we were pulled together like moths to a flame. On the final night of the five-day camp, we were given time to get together as one large group and socialize before returning to our busy lives back in the city. As usual, Ryan and I were chatting and taking small, friendly jabs at each other—both verbal and physical. All of a sudden, Ryan buried his face in my neck and snorted while pretending to take a bite out of me. He couldn't have known this, but that was something my dad used to do to me when I was a young girl while we were play wrestling.

Overwhelming nostalgia welled up inside of me. My heart was bursting—both for a sweet memory with my dad and for this guy who had just tapped into that.

"Hey." Ryan smiled as he threw his arm around my shoulder. "I really want to sit with you on the way back to Buenos Aires."

I smiled back and looked up at him. "Me too."

In that moment, I realized that I had slowly fallen in love. It caught me by surprise. So much so that all I could do was memorialize this epiphany as a one-line entry in my journal:

7–21–07

Of course I'll write later, but I must say this one thing:

I think I might be in love with Ryan.

Understanding that my heart had grown to care for and value Ryan in a way I wasn't expecting, I knew I had to make a move. In two short weeks, Ryan would be leaving Argentina to head back to Tennessee.

I needed to know if he felt the same before he was potentially gone forever. There were no guarantees, but the idea of never knowing how he felt was not an option.

I decided to talk to him one night as he walked me to a nearby corner to catch a cab home. It was late, but the city streets were still buzzing with passing cars. We walked past people out for a nighttime stroll. I kept trying to think of a way to start the conversation. My nerves nearly got the best of me, but I finally managed to blurt out, "Are we more than friends?"

Oof. That was less than eloquent.

"You want to have the DTR?" he asked me without missing a beat.

"DTR?" I repeated, confused. He didn't stop walking, so neither did I.

"Yeah, the conversation where we 'define the relationship.'"

"Oh. Well, I guess I do." We walked a little further until we got to a corner where we knew we'd be able to get a taxi to stop.

At that point, Ryan—who would soon be entering a program to receive his Master's in Marriage and Family Therapy (MFT)—turned toward me and got extremely close to my face. I felt my cheeks burning, and I wasn't sure what he was about to do. He started to put some of his budding therapy skills to work.

"If I like you, my eyes will dilate. It won't be something I can control; it will be completely involuntary. Look into my eyes. What do you see?"

Honestly, I couldn't see anything. It was too dark. I wasn't sure how to answer, and I was confused as to why he was making this a guessing game. I just smiled and whispered his name.

"See?" he continued. "No dilation."

Yikes.

Embarrassed, but more in shock at how much of a nonevent my pseudo declaration of love was for him, I just sheepishly nodded and forced a small smile. Ryan pulled me into a warm embrace.

"I'm glad we had this talk," he said.

This really wasn't a conversation, but OK. Seconds later, we hailed a passing cab and it carried me home.

I learned years later that Ryan was betraying his true feelings that night. He'd grown to care deeply for me, but by the time he realized it and I had said something to him, he only had two weeks left in Argentina. Thinking it unwise to explore a relationship with me right before putting thousands of miles between us, he made the unilateral decision to shut things down before they could start. He considered it the mature thing to do and was proud of himself for putting practicality before personal desire.

My pride was a little hurt during the cab ride home that night, but I found that I bounced back rather quickly. I wasn't a stranger to awkward moments such as these. Both a blessing and a curse, I've always been bold in seeking the answers to questions, even if I suspect that I won't like what I find out. My Defining The Relationship "talk" with Ryan was hardly the first time I had brought up my feelings with someone that I liked. In high school, the results of these talks were unfavorable 100% of the time.

It was actually something that perplexed and worried me if I thought about it too much. When it came to my crushes, they came in all shapes, sizes, and shades. It was easy to find something attractive about most people whether it be physical, emotional, or intellectual. I soon discovered, however, that I wasn't palatable for most boys.

Looking back on it now, I can see that I carried myself differently than a lot of the other Black girls in school. Omaha was and still is very racially segregated. I didn't grow up where most of the Black families lived. I wasn't raised in an over-policed neighborhood. I had easy access to any sought-after conveniences or amenities (think movie theaters, multiple grocery stores, shopping malls). While I dealt with plenty of ignorance for being the only Black person many of my peers knew, I was allowed to grow up free from the burden of living within the redlined North Omaha community that racism had built. That type of carefreeness translated into a lightheartedness that I think was something Black guys liked. They liked my playful disposition, but ultimately, I was "too strange", "too weird", "too goofy", or "too white" for them to actually consider dating me.

For white guys, I was no match for the white girls we went to school with who met the culturally-accepted beauty standards with ease—straight hair, slender nose, light eyes, small butt, and, of course, fair skin.

As for the boys from other ethnic groups, I'll never really know what kept them away. But as an adult, I've come to learn that anti-Blackness is not uniquely American. It spans the globe. I can't help but wonder if conversations at home influenced how they viewed me at school.

In any event, Defining The Relationship with Ryan shed light on the type of connection we had, and for that, I could be grateful. I was clear about where we stood. Luckily, his go-with-the-flow attitude took away any awkwardness that should have been there when I saw him the next day. If he wasn't going to be awkward, neither would I. I decided to savor what little time I had left with him during what was turning out to be one of the most memorable times of my life.

Three days later, in the home where Ryan and Wes were staying, we stayed up talking late into the night as was our usual custom. Wes, recognizing that he was fading fast, gave us hugs and retreated to his bedroom.

"Are you tired, Jenn?" Ryan asked as he looked at me.

"No, surprisingly."

"Do you want to watch a movie?"

"Sure!"

After settling on *The Departed* with its star-studded cast, Ryan got up and put the disc in the DVD player. On his way back to the couch where I was sitting, he turned off the lights. The room was dark, aside from the glow of the TV screen. He plopped down next to me—his shoulder and thigh touching mine, leaving no sliver of space in between us. I enjoyed being this close, but had to keep my thoughts and feelings in check. I knew where he stood.

A few minutes into the movie, I felt Ryan shifting in his seat quite a bit. I acted like nothing was happening, but slyly watched out of my peripheral view. Without warning, I felt two fingers tickling my side.

In a flash I leaned away from him. "Ryan, what are you doing? I don't like to be tickled," I said, slightly panicky.

"Well, that's too bad for you," he quipped before launching into a full-on tickle attack. My head was clouded with confusion as my body reacted to the tickling. I was used to us being physical with each other, but we hadn't been quite so physical before. Recognizing I was losing the battle, I curled up into a ball to cover my most ticklish spots as he hovered over me.

"Jenn, *tengo muchas ganas de besarte*." (Jenn, I really feel like kissing you.)

It felt like time had stopped. *Did he just say what I think he said?*

I gave a nervous giggle and found his eyes. "Then do it."

Two weeks later, as I was saying goodbye to him at the airport, I told him that I wasn't the kind of girl who was going to leave my own adventure to follow a guy. I didn't feel like my journey in Argentina was done yet. I told him this, and it was true, but what I didn't tell him was that I was scared. I was scared that once he got back to his life in Tennessee, he would forget about me and the strong connection we had. "Just wait for me as long as you can," I begged him through my tears.

"I can wait forever; I just hope I don't have to," he replied. I felt such comfort from those words. He would wait for me.

With that, he boarded the plane that would carry him thousands of miles away . . . and I was left behind in the airport, quietly weeping.

Ryan and I stayed connected, alleviating my fears of being forgotten. We tried to talk every day. This was before the days of video chats. Google had just come out with Google Talk that allowed us to make phone calls from our computers—the zenith of technology! In the beginning, our chats consisted of me keeping him updated on the people we both knew in Buenos Aires while he told me about his life in Tennessee. We missed each other a lot and didn't skip an opportunity to let one another know. Saying "I love you" was still in our daily routine, but it had taken on a new meaning—its traditional meaning—between us.

I was so excited about what was developing and I wanted a unique way to show Ryan. I decided to film myself singing Stevie Wonder's *For Once In My Life* and send it to him through Facebook. These were the early days of Facebook, before I, and most people, understood the public nature of posting to someone's wall (now known as the Facebook feed). I proudly posted it one night and went to bed eager to get his reaction the next day.

When I woke up the next morning, I logged on to Facebook to see if he had seen my video. I was mortified to find that not only did he see it, but so did all of his friends as well as my own. There was comment after comment with heart emojis and all sorts of questions. "Ohhhh, who is this Ryan guy?" "Awww, this is so cute!" I even got a private message from a college friend jabbing in jest that she always knew I'd end up with a white guy. There was also a Facebook Group invitation. The group was called Loving My Baby. The invite was from Ryan.

> Hey Babe, I made a private group where we can post all of our gushy messages to each other without other people seeing. Loved the video by the way! Love you!

A few months later, my time in Buenos Aires came to a close. I would be lying if I said my decision to leave wasn't heavily influenced by the fact that my relationship with Ryan was deepening every day.

Ryan and I got to know each other through hours and hours of conversation. In that time, we shared beautiful words, ambitious dreams, and a longing to be near one another. Whatever loving feelings I had experienced up to that point toward other guys paled in comparison to the explosion happening in my heart daily just at the thought of Ryan. I remember thinking to myself one day, *I'm going to marry this guy.* That was the final push I needed. I bought my return ticket to the U.S. and spent the week of Thanksgiving with Ryan in Tennessee before making my way home to Omaha.

It takes more than love to turn the page and start a new chapter in life

To this day, I joke and say that I would still be in Buenos Aires if I hadn't met Ryan. I enjoyed living in Argentina more than I could have imagined—I never wanted to leave. But there was something different about Ryan and how carefree I felt with him. I liked who I was when I was with him. I could be my unfiltered self and he was not only OK with that, he loved it. Unlike the boys from high school, I wasn't too much of anything for him. I felt seen, appreciated, beautiful—loved. When I allowed myself to dream with him, we envisioned a whole life opening up that we could create together. With him, I saw the promise of a commitment and dedication to helping one another reach our goals. I saw something worth pursuing.

Chapter 2

Will Love Be Enough?

Four months of daily phone calls and a couple of weekend visits later, Ryan and I were engaged to be married. We certainly didn't have it all figured out, but the "big picture" view looked good. Now, looking back, I cringe to think about the things we didn't know about each other. At the time, that just didn't seem like a big deal.

"Hey, Jenn, how old are you, by the way?"

"Oh my gosh!" I laughed. "I'm twenty-two."

"Oh, okay. I wasn't too far off."

"What do you mean? How old did you think I was?"

"After you left the ring store yesterday, the ladies at the counter commented on how young you look. They asked me how old you were."

"And what did you say?" This was going to be interesting.

He shrugged. "I said twenty-three or twenty-four, but I wasn't sure."

I laughed. "Nope. Only twenty-two. You're twenty-five, right?"

Our 365 days of engagement looked a lot like our eight months of dating because we were living in different cities—Ryan was down south in Bristol and I was in Omaha for a few months before moving to Chicago for grad school. We talked endlessly on the phone and tried to see each other as often as two broke students could afford (which ended up being about every four or five weeks). Yes, we were young and naive; but we were being as thoughtful and as practical as two young twentysomethings could be. We were serious about our relationship, and we were serious about each other. We hadn't had the opportunity to get to know each other's friends or family, but we figured we had our whole lives to do that.

Why is that detail important? Because over the past several years of my marriage, I have firmly stated that had we taken things more slowly, had I gotten a chance to get to know my husband's family, we never would have made it to the altar. I have spoken those words in moments of pain and in moments of gratitude and awe. We have four beautiful children who I can't imagine this world without. I consider it a gift that our pre-marital life consisted of weekend visits away from his family where we just focused on each other; it would have been a real tragedy for society if our kids were never given the opportunity to make their mark on it.

The Ryan I met and fell in love with was a Ryan who, only two years prior to us meeting, had moved away from his family and all that he had ever known in Fargo, North Dakota. My Ryan was a transplant to a Tennessee college campus and was becoming accustomed to an environment of greater diversity in people, thoughts, and experiences. He realized that there was a whole world beyond what he had been exposed to, and that he had things to learn.

In Tennessee, he learned that it was okay to be a gentleman and show courtesy to others—not to project weakness onto the other person, as he had previously thought, but rather as an act of service. He came into contact with people who'd had completely different experiences than his own. He formed friendships with people who had emigrated from other countries, spoke different languages, and grew up with different faith traditions.

Some of the students in his Marriage and Family Therapy cohort came from economically privileged backgrounds, while others did not. Their paths to financial stability were varied, and how they showed their economic independence differed from what Ryan was used to. One day, one of his Black female classmates walked in proudly sporting a new purse. It was comprised of a patchwork of different patterns.

Ryan noticed it right away. "Mariah, I like your new purse!"

"Thanks!" Mariah said as she smiled and rotated the bag to show it to him from all angles.

"That's so cool! Did you make it yourself?"

According to the way Ryan described the situation to me later that evening on the phone, he noticed that the air was sucked out of the room from the moment he said that. Mariah got an offended look on her face. "It's a Coach purse," she huffed as she quickly walked to the other side of the room to find a seat. Ryan was puzzled—he didn't understand what he had said to change the dynamic so fast.

"Ryan!" I exclaimed, shocked. "You said that about her Coach bag?"

"Yes..." he said, hesitantly. "It was a compliment. I really liked it."

"Babe, you probably offended Mariah. Eek," I said, cringing. "I can't believe you said that."

"I don't get why this is a big deal."

"Coach is a really expensive brand of purses," I began. "Maybe it's a big deal that she was able to afford that, and you basically reduced its significance by implying it was something she could have thrown together herself."

"Oh, gosh. I didn't even realize," he said softly as what I had just told him sank in.

It was moments like these that expanded Ryan's understanding of the varied human experience. What he considered a compliment was received as an underhanded jab at one's status symbol. But Ryan didn't cower in shame. He listened to my words and trusted the differing perspective I offered. I loved that about him.

My Ryan became the Ryan I knew away from all that *he* knew and all that knew him. Being a person who struggles to maintain deeply connected relationships of any kind (ours being the exception), My Ryan became a different Ryan without his family or friends realizing that he was no longer *their* Ryan—the Ryan they had always known. He was gaining new perspectives and hearing new ideas without ever connecting with friends and family back home. They weren't seeing in real time that Ryan was being stretched in his thinking and how this was shaping him. In hindsight, I think this is why I would come to be seen as having a much larger influence over him than I actually had. From the vantage point of those he knew back in Fargo, the only thing that had changed about *their* Ryan was that he met a girl and fell in love.

Pre-Jenn, *their* Ryan was a bit crass and didn't bat an eyelash at off-color remarks. A frequent listener to Rush Limbaugh and other voices on the conservative Talk Radio platform, *their* Ryan was "black and white" in his thinking, with little tolerance for shades of gray. *Their* Ryan was content with surface-level relationships. His best friends were the ones he spent years sitting next to while playing videogames, but he couldn't tell you the first thing about their personal lives. *Their* Ryan was directionless, but a nice enough guy who avoided conflict.

By the time we met, Ryan had been in Bristol for two years, having completed his Masters in Christian ministry. He saw the program through to the end, but he didn't want to be a traditional pulpit minister. Wanting to serve people in a meaningful way, he applied to the Marriage and Family Therapy program, which he started immediately after leaving Buenos Aires. During his first Masters program, he met young men and women engaging in meaningful dialogue and vulnerably sharing their questions and ideas about life. That made a profound impact on Ryan. He started to leave his polarizing "black and white" viewpoint behind and began recognizing the importance of nuance.

The Ryan I met was always up for a thoughtful conversation. He wanted to be challenged and engage in spirited dialogue—verbal sparring, he called it. In those early days, I wondered to myself why he wasn't a philosophy major. He had thoughts and ideas that he could expound upon for days. I'll never forget when he started to explain to me his political stance. He made his argument for why he wasn't completely conservative, nor liberal, nor Democrat, nor Republican (which, for him, were four distinct categories—an idea I had not yet been introduced to). Reminding me a lot of my analytically-minded white best friend, Jessica, I remember thinking they would be perfect for one another. I briefly considered introducing them to one another; in hindsight, I'm glad they didn't meet until after Ryan and I were solidly committed to one another.

When I realized my feelings for Ryan, and then his for me, it hit me that our relationship wouldn't carry on in the comfort of Buenos Aires forever. I would go back to feeling the weight of being a Black woman in the U.S. If I visited him, which I was determined to do, it would mean going to a small town in Tennessee. For better or worse, the South doesn't have the greatest reputation when it comes to race relations considering our country's racial past. The thought of traveling south made me nervous, and heading to a small town made me even more nervous. I wasn't sure how diverse it would be. It had been my experience that the citizens of small towns don't tend to have a lot of firsthand exposure to people or ideas that are different—and I considered being Black to be different enough.

That's when I began looking at our relationship through the lens of race. I wasn't considering his race when thinking about whether or not I wanted him to be mine and me to be his; that was a resounding "Yes!" But I did have some nagging thoughts about what life would be like back in the States being in such a close relationship with someone white—someone who hadn't had some of the same experiences I'd had.

I was well-adept at being the only Black person in the room and having my skin color be the only indication that I was different. I learned from an early age to fit in, and usually felt comfortable in my surroundings until someone *else* pointed out that I was different.

I was accustomed to getting uncomfortable questions and comments from white people regarding my race and culture. From a friend's younger brother asking, "Did you know you're Black?" to being called an Oreo by a classmate ("Get it? You're Black on the outside, but white on the inside!") to a customer at my high school job remarking, "You speak like a white person," I'd heard it all. It didn't matter how many times I heard it. I was shocked every time that someone would say these things to another person. It took years for me to begin to formulate responses to these types of comments, and even longer to get the courage to speak them aloud in the moment.

Still, I recognize that my childhood experiences with race were better than those of other people. I went almost my entire childhood only having to deal with ignorant or prejudiced slights. Sure, there were those times when I was next in line at a store and purposefully overlooked by the cashier. I'd had those experiences where someone's facial expression, when seeing me in a public place, made it unmistakably clear that my very presence was offensive. I knew in my soul what was going on, but the indirect nature of incidents like those left room for doubt to creep in. *Was I really experiencing what I thought I was experiencing? Maybe it's not me, it's them. They're having a bad day and they would treat anybody like that.* It wasn't until I was seventeen that I was on the receiving end of an overtly racist encounter.

It was the last Friday in June, during the summer leading into my senior year. I had big plans and I felt on top of the world. That night, I would be meeting up with several friends from school at Memorial Park in Omaha for an outdoor concert and fireworks show. It was for the annual Celebrate America concert to commemorate the Fourth of July. Creedence Clearwater Revival was performing that night, and as a teenager who listened to oldies music nonstop on 99.9 KGOR, I was pumped. Because traffic in the immediate vicinity of the park was going to be congested, I drove to Jessica's house in the nearby Dundee neighborhood. The plan was to leave my car there and walk together to meet up with the rest of our friends.

The weather was perfect. It was warm outside, the sun was shining in all its glory, and there was a gentle breeze moving through the tree branches. I was driving my black Chrysler Cirrus through the streets of Dundee, windows all the way down, head bopping to my music. Just around the corner from Jessica's house, I pulled up to the infamously tricky six-way stop—the point where six roads converge, and all cars are halted by stop signs. I didn't love that intersection and avoided it when I could. It was hard for me to keep track of the cars and know for certain who had the right of way.

Today, the six-way stop couldn't be avoided. I sat at the stop sign, watching the different cars around me make their way across the intersection. I had my right hand on the wheel, while my left elbow hung out of the window as I rested my arm. I started to get into the rhythm of the music, so I extended my left arm and began tapping the beat with my hand on the exterior of the driver side door. I kept looking around at the different drivers and felt like it might be my turn. I made eye contact with the driver to my right—an older man who smiled and waved me on, signaling it was my turn to go. I smiled and waved back before starting to accelerate.

HONK!

I slammed to a stop at the sound of someone laying on their horn. I heard screeching tires and looked on in confusion as a gray minivan peeled through the intersection. My head turned as my gaze followed the car. The driver, a white woman, rolled down her window, looked right at me with the ugliest sneer imaginable, and screamed, "Dumb nigger!" as she drove by.

I turned to face forward.

Keep tapping your hand.

I could feel tears welling up in my eyes and willed them not to fall with all my might.

Don't let it show. Don't let them know that affected you.

No one at the six-way stop moved. It was as if time stood still. After what was only seconds but felt like minutes, I let my foot off the brake and made my way to Jessica's house.

I pulled up to the curb, rolled up my windows, put the car in park, and activated the emergency brake. Then I lost it. I brought my hands up to my face and violently sobbed. If someone had seen me, they would have thought I had just lost someone dear to me. And in a way, I had—me. I lost a big piece of my innocence that day. I didn't try to stop the tears as I started screaming to no one in particular, "Why did she scream that at me? What did I do to deserve that? It was my turn! He told me it was my turn! Why did that have to happen to me?" It went on like this for fifteen minutes or so. Every few minutes,

I'd glance up at Jessica's house to make sure no one saw me through the windows. When my tears had finally stopped, I sat for another ten minutes, patting my cheeks and fanning my eyes dry. I took deep breaths and eventually calmed down. I gave myself one more look in the rearview mirror, fixed any out of place hairs, and got out of my car. I walked up to the porch like nothing happened. I vowed to take the pain and shame I felt to the grave. *No one ever has to know.* I knocked on the door. Jessica opened it up almost immediately.

I flashed a smile. "Hey! Sorry I'm late!"

"I was starting to get worried. Is everything OK?" she asked.

I bounced past her. "Oh yeah! Girl, please. You know traffic around here is crazy!"

What happened at that six-way stop would dictate my behavior around white people for years—*years*. After that, I became very fearful of ever upsetting another white person with my mistakes, afraid that I would give them a reason to call me that word. I never wanted to be called that again. In that one moment, at that six-way stop, the confidence I had in myself to navigate white spaces was destroyed.

By the time Ryan came into my life, enough time had passed without incident that I no longer feared being called such a vile word. I did, however, assume that's what white people were saying about me in their heads when I saw those looks of disgust cross their faces or whenever I made a mistake in their presence. I never felt that fear with Ryan, but I did start to wonder about the circles Ryan moved in. I started to wonder if he could even conceive of the types of experiences I'd had.

He did realize my daily experiences were different from his own. In one of our many emails exchanges while I was still in Argentina and he was back in Tennessee, Ryan talked about delving into themes of racism in America.

I just finished a conference on racism, and I am more convinced than ever that change needs to happen, especially in the churches. I now have a new life goal: racial reconciliation in the church. I hope you will join me.

I'm resisting giving myself a facepalm now, but at the time, reading that provided me with such relief. Ryan was already seeking out opportunities to learn about and discuss race and racism on his own! And I cringe to admit this, but it was that snippet of email that suggested to me that our different ethnicities weren't going to be a giant hurdle for us.

But there were moments prior to us getting married when it was clear to me that Ryan still had learning to do and that his family lacked cultural awareness. I remember when I asked Ryan about his family's first impressions of me. He revealed that his dad's first words after seeing my picture were "nice tan." And when his grandma was relaying to a family friend what little she knew about this mystery girl Ryan had met in Argentina, she told her friend that I was brown and from Kansas.

"I can't believe she said you were from Kansas!" he said, laughing.

"She could have said I was from Kentucky for all I care," I said indignantly. I was surprised he didn't hear what I heard in that statement. "That's not what was wrong with that statement," I said more quietly to myself.

Even with that red flag slowly ascending the flagpole, I was more concerned with his mom's lack of boundaries and brash intrusions into our affairs as a couple. I'll never forget the first time I spoke with her on the phone. It was during the week I stopped in Bristol after leaving Buenos Aires.

"So, Ryan said you're going to grad school next year."

"Yes, I'll start in August, so I have about nine months."

"He said you're going to get a masters in Spanish," she said.

"Yeah, that's right. I think I want to focus on bilingualism and second language acquisition."

"Spanish is good," she started, "but you should really get an MBA. I told all my kids they should go to business school."

For the record, I went on to get my master's in Spanish linguistics, and none of her children have an MBA. When I got off the phone with her, Ryan could see I was taken aback by something his mom had said.

"What's with the look?"

"I mean . . . that was the first conversation I've ever had with her, and she told me I should change my career path."

He laughed. "Yep, that's my mom."

Boy, was he ever right! I didn't have much contact with my future mother-in-law, but every time I did, she inserted her opinion on what and how things should be done. This was especially true once Ryan and I were engaged and planning our wedding.

"I know a destination wedding sounds like a fun idea. But if you have one, no one will go."

"Summer isn't the greatest time for a wedding. You should think about moving the date. We have nephews who have baseball tournaments, and it will be hard for them to come."

"Don't get married while you're still long-distance. You don't want to do that."

Early on, I pegged Ryan's parents (more so his mom than his dad) as people I did not want to do life around, and I told him so. I had never been around two people whose main conversation topic was to criticize their own friends and family members. Ryan also had a younger brother, nine years his junior, who still lived at home. I'd sometimes look his way in the wake of one of their many critical comments, and he never seemed phased. This was what he was used to.

Thankfully, we were rarely around them geographically. They lived in Fargo, Ryan was down in Tennessee, and I was in Omaha for nearly a year before eventually moving to Chicago for grad school. We were back and forth between the cities where *we* lived; we had no reason to ever meet up in North Dakota. Ryan and I managed to sail through our engagement period without getting to know his family's understanding of race or their capabilities to wade through racially tense situations.

Ryan, on the other hand, was able to get to know my parents. In those months before moving to Chicago, he made a handful of trips to Omaha to visit me while I was living at their house. And because his sister, Jewel, was a short distance away in Lincoln, I was able to meet her early on when she drove up to see us. On that first meeting, we drove downtown, grabbed a bite to eat, and spent the afternoon walking around. True to what Ryan had said, it felt like meeting a version of myself. We had a lot in common, and the conversation never waned between us. After having met Ryan's parents, this meeting was a breath of fresh air. This is what I was hoping for—instant connections, conversations with ease, a feeling of warmth.

When we'd had enough of walking around, we hopped in the car and Ryan drove us home—his sister called shotgun and I happily plopped myself in the backseat.

"I've decided to give up eating skittles," Jewel announced. "I want to get healthier."

I gasped, shocked, and reached toward the front seat to touch her shoulder. "Even the red ones?"

She turned around to face me. "Yes, even the red ones. It's all or nothing."

"Wow. That's bold," I said admiringly. "Truly."

I got a glimpse of Ryan in the rearview mirror. I could see the smile of satisfaction on his face as his sister and I moved on to the next topic without missing a beat.

My dad had reservations early on about my relationship with Ryan. For him, it was all moving way too quickly. From his perspective, he had put me on a plane to Argentina only to have me come back six months later claiming I had found the person I was going to marry. He thought I was too young and too naïve to already commit myself to someone for the rest of my life.

But Ryan had a loyal ally in my mom. From the days when I was still in Argentina and I told her about him, they started to get to know one another apart from me through phone calls. Before they met face to face, she and Ryan had already established that he would call her Mom. It did not take her long to see what I saw in him. She saw how easy it was to talk to this down-to-earth young man, and she was determined to support us. Though my dad had given Ryan his blessing to ask me to marry him, behind closed doors his reaction to our engagement mirrored that of a man whose dog had died.

The morning after Ryan proposed, I sat at my mom's feet while she was putting on her makeup in the bathroom mirror. "Mom, what is his problem?" I asked, tearfully exasperated. "It's not because Ryan's white, is it?"

My mom flashed that "are-you-serious?" look that only a mom can give. "You know we don't care about that. He's just having a hard time. You're his baby—his only girl. He wants you to have everything you want in the world, and he's scared that Ryan is going to get in the way of that."

I knew she was right. Even when I asked it, I knew this wasn't about race. Ryan was not the first, nor would he be the last, white person to marry into our family. I understood how precious I was to my dad, but I was frustrated that his sentimentality and fears were getting in the way of what should have been a purely happy time for me.

"Well, Ryan is here to stay. Dad can't keep acting like this. You both got to choose who you wanted to be with. I'm making my choice."

Knowing me and seeing the resolve in my eyes, my mom saw that as her cue to step in. She went to my dad.

"Don't make Jenn choose. She won't choose us."

That was all she needed to say. And because my dad loves me more than life itself, he yielded. He chose to welcome Ryan into our family, and his heart quickly softened toward the man I had chosen to soon become my husband. Ryan wouldn't know about my dad's apprehension about us getting married or my willingness to give my parents an ultimatum until I told him years later.

Once we got married, we made a more concerted effort to visit Ryan's family. Ryan wanted them to get to know this woman he had fallen in love with. He wanted the joining of our families to be seamless. He even shared with me that it was his dream to live in a cul-de-sac and have each member of his family own one of the houses so that we could experience life together.

I agreed with the effort to see them more frequently. In my own family, I had seen countless examples of healthy, thriving in-law relationships. We, as a family, took it very seriously when we gained a new relationship through marriage. They became our family—my brothers' wives were my sisters and my parents' daughters. Many times, I witnessed my dad come to the aid of my mom's parents as if they were his own. To this day, my mom still talks about how she had the best mother-in-law in the world. It was this idea of having an additional set of loving parents, additional siblings, and even additional extended family that excited me. I hadn't had the best first impression with our short exchanges, but I knew I hadn't had the chance to spend real quality time with them. That needed to change.

It was during those extended times with Ryan's family that it became clear to me how much of a detriment the lack of exposure to other cultures can be for a person—or in this case, an entire family. Beforehand, the long-distance meddling by his mom had overshadowed the occasional hints at racial insensitivities from his family. But now, little comments from Ryan's family here and there left me feeling very uncomfortable.

"So, can you explain the hair thing?"

"Do Black people really not like to swim?"

"I knew a Black girl once."

"This may be racist, but I just love caramel babies."

In those initial months, I was in shock. Shock gave way to an exhaustion and a feeling of anxiousness when I knew I was going to spend time with Ryan's family. And even though I was sure that he was different, there was a corner of my mind that harbored doubt, a fragment of my heart that lodged fear. Doubts and fears that I had somehow missed the true nature of my new husband's character.

Had I unknowingly welcomed the ignorance I dealt with in society into my familial sphere? I had so many thoughts. So many questions. I vacillated between confusion and full-on panic.

How did Ryan come from this family? While Ryan was a direct person, he was capable of speaking in nuanced language when a situation called for it. I didn't get the sense at all that his family knew how to do that.

He doesn't share these thoughts, does he?

How did I not know?

I began to consider myself a fool to think that our dating and engagement period could go so smoothly and stay that way.

What am I going to do?

How often do we have to visit North Dakota?

Is this just the older generations, or are the cousins equally as ignorant?
This is when I started the risk assessment by categorizing the people in his family as safe or not safe.

What am I going to do?

Do they realize that they're talking to a Black person?

WHAT AM I GOING TO DO?

The uncomfortable comments I got from Ryan's family far outnumbered the times I actually went to him with my discomfort. I was a young newlywed enamored with her husband who didn't want to rock the boat. I didn't want to create conflict so early on in our marriage over some people we wouldn't see but once or twice a year. On a deeper level, I think I was afraid to have any conversation with Ryan that would confirm my fears that maybe he wasn't so different from his family. I'm typically a very good-natured person, so I became skilled at flashing a tight-lipped smile and making a quick exit in the face of uncomfortable questions and comments.

The solace I found in being with my own family became more pronounced in those early years and I came to fervently seek it whenever I spent time with Ryan's family. My parents' house has always been the hub, a place to have dinners or host a game night with extended family. Some of us sit around the kitchen table talking and laughing, while others sit in the family room watching a sports game on TV. Ryan usually sat in the family room trying to learn more about the sports my family enjoyed. I tended to sit in the kitchen talking.

"How's married life?" was a general question I would often get.

I'd smile a genuine smile. "It's good—no complaints."

"Jenny-Jenn," started my uncle (the only one I allow to call me that), "what's it like in Fargo?"

"Flat." I laughed and shook my head. "I don't see too much of it. We're usually just at Ryan's parents' house."

My aunt leaned in. "What is his family like? Are they—" She cocked her head and arched her eyebrows.

I knew what she was asking. She was asking me if being with Ryan's family was what we would come to refer to in later years as a "Get Out" moment (in reference to the 2017 Jordan Peele movie by the same name). She was asking me if it was uncomfortable being the only Black person around all of his white family.

"They're cool," I assured her. "Super nice."

My aunt relaxed and changed her tone. "Ok. That's good to hear. They seemed nice at the wedding."

Keep the peace, Jenn. Just keep the peace. I didn't want anyone to know that I was struggling with Ryan's family. I didn't want my own family to worry about me. As for Ryan, I considered it my gift to him (a gift he never asked for, nor knew I was giving) to grin and bear my way through short stints with his relatives so that he could live under the guise that I was fitting into his family as nicely as he fit into mine. But nothing built on sand stands forever.

It takes more than love to harmoniously integrate into a new family

At the time, I marveled at how Ryan's family could look me in the eye and make the comments or ask the questions they did. For some of them, I was their opportunity to have all of their burning questions about "all things Black" answered. I was the access to Black culture and the Black experience they had never had before. I also recognize that others in my new family thought they were relating to me or getting to know me. I am not making an excuse for their ignorant questions and comments, but it's important to recognize what they were actually trying to do, especially if you're a white person reading this now and rolling your eyes at the indiscretions of Ryan's family. You may fall into the same trap yourself.

Honing in on what makes a person different in a conversation with them is not the same as relating to or showing interest in them. When Ryan's family went out of their way to mention the one Black person they knew or asked me questions to either confirm or deny a stereotype they'd heard about, I didn't feel welcomed. I can only speak for myself. But when someone does this to me, the only thing it accomplishes is highlighting the fact that they see me as someone (or some*thing*) different.

My initial interactions with Ryan's family would have been more positive if they hadn't tried to prove to me all they knew (or didn't know) about Black people. I would have preferred them to keep their questions at bay, first allowing for trust to build. It's hard to be the newcomer into any family, and it makes it doubly hard when the interactions highlight the differences instead of the similarities.

I feel like I'm stating the obvious, but it's OK to get to know a person simply for who they are—not the group you think they represent. As you get to know someone more deeply, if you've presented yourself as safe and open-minded, you'll be welcomed into the deeper story of who that person is.

Chapter 3

The Christmas from Hell

Christmas is one of my favorite times of the year. My earliest memories are of my childhood home decorated in every nook and cranny. My mom proudly displayed her Department 56 Dickens' Village that stretched along several tables—cobblestone streets covered in artificial snow, Christmas carolers, ice skaters on a pond, a train station, and, my favorite, The Old Curiosity Shop. The mantle was filled with nearly a hundred Black Santas, ranging from round and jolly to tall and slender, in every beautiful brown hue imaginable (a collection that took years for her to build). Even my dad got in on the decorating action. His little red bows adorned every knob on our kitchen cabinets and led the way upstairs on every spindle of the stairway banister. It was magical.

The sounds and smells of Christmas in our home were just as vivid as the sights. My mom had an array of wintertime candles that she would burn (a tradition that I've continued in my own home). The one that sticks out most in my mind is "holiday peppermint." The scent of that candle swirled around and danced with the aroma of my mom's homemade mac and cheese, honey-baked ham, collard greens, and sweet potato pie. My mouth waters just thinking about it.

To top it off, the scene was not complete without Christmas music playing. Whether it be the Winans family, Babyface, or Mariah Carey (my personal favorite), soulful renditions of our favorite carols played throughout the month of December. Our home was the place to be during the Christmas season. When I got married, I was sad to realize that I would have to give up some of my Christmases at home to celebrate with Ryan's family.

Our first Christmas with my new family happened a little before our second anniversary. Ryan and I were living in Chicago, working our first adult jobs, and still just a family of two. We were getting into our groove as a couple, and life was good. The plan that year was to celebrate Christmas at Jewel's home in Las Vegas instead of braving the blustery winter of North Dakota. It would include Ryan's entire nuclear family plus his grandma, the matriarch. I had never been to Vegas before, nor had I ever spent Christmas in a warmer climate. In general, I was looking forward to it.

We landed in Las Vegas, excited to be there and to shed our winter coats. At baggage claim, my sister-in-law was waiting for us with hugs. True to form, she and Ryan lit up at the sight of each other and ran into one another's arms for a prolonged embrace. Only a little over a year apart in age, the two of them have a close bond, and their childish antics are often reignited when together.

Once the entire family had flown in, we caravanned to the house. The "kids" (Ryan, his younger brother, his sister, and me) were together in his sister's car. Ryan claimed the front passenger seat, and I plopped down in back with his brother.

Jewel talked a mile a minute as she pointed out different points of interest on the way to her house while simultaneously asking us questions about activities that we would like to do over the next few days.

"Are you guys into Thai food? If you take a right down this street, there's this great little restaurant that my coworkers and I go to. And if we jump on the highway here, it's not too far from Red Rock Canyon if you think that is something you'd want to do."

In between pointing out the sights and trying to plan our time together, we jumped from topic to topic as we caught up on one another's lives. Eventually, someone brought up genealogy. Although a subject of keen personal interest for me, I often come to the conversation at a deficit. For people of African descent, genealogy can be inaccessible beyond a certain point. Yes, there are Black people who can trace their roots for hundreds of years; but many of us hit dead ends once we reach the time period when our ancestors were enslaved for the simple fact that we were considered property, not people. Historic records of enslavement may not identify the people by name, but only by their sex and approximate age, if that. Surnames were not their own, but given to them by the enslaver. For anyone to trace their family takes a fair bit of detective work. For those with a history of slavery, the task is even harder.

Ryan's family lore is much more traceable and something of a hobby for his mom. From the back seat, I commented that I could only go back so far in my history and was unable to determine which African country my family descended from. I regret ever having said something.

At a red light, Ryan's sister turned around and faced me in the backseat. "Let's try to figure out which country you came from!"

Their little brother turned toward me. "Well, her eyes are pretty set apart. But her brow line doesn't protrude that much."

"Yeah, I see it," Jewel concurred. "And her nose looks like those kids from Ethiopia. You know, those kids who have the big bellies because they're starving?"

"Oh yeah. Totally," he agreed.

Ryan's brother and sister took my declaration of not knowing my ancestors' country of origin as an invitation to not only study my facial features, but to make assertions about which African country these physical traits tied me to. Their scrutiny led them to the conclusion that my family must come from Ethiopia. They were taking gross generalizations and flippantly connecting me to a place that neither one of them had visited. I doubted they even knew anyone from Ethiopia. Honestly, it wouldn't have mattered if they did.

I felt objectified, ostracized, and even more shame than I'd felt before at how my ancestral history prohibited me from really knowing where my roots lay. I was hurt by the attempt of my "white saviors" to reunite me with my interrupted lineage. I was angry that, in the end, their guess was as good as mine.

Hurt and in disbelief, I looked to my husband for recognition of and protection from this absurdity. I looked toward him, in the front seat, expecting his eyes to meet mine with a similar look of disbelief and pain. I expected him to stop the conversation dead in its tracks, even if it made the rest of the ride home (or the rest of the weekend, for that matter) painfully awkward. But that didn't happen.

My eyes were instead met with the back of Ryan's head. I wasn't sure if he had heard the conversation or if his mind was elsewhere, captivated by the lights of the Vegas strip that we drove through on the way to the house. It was as if he wasn't even in the car.

Left alone to show my disapproval of the conversation that had just transpired, I said to his sister the only honest thing that came to mind: "It's scary to think that someone like you is in the legal profession."

In defense of his sister, Ryan's brother said, "Wow. That's harsh."

And what you both just said to me wasn't? I had no more words.

And this was just the drive home from the airport.

This exchange, though brief, was impactful, because my guard was not previously up around Ryan's siblings. I had already classified the older members of his family as unsafe. I'd had to field enough ignorant comments and questions to know they were to be avoided whenever possible. Now I felt like I was surrounded and forced to have a wall up even around my contemporaries in this family. Even more troubling was my husband's silence. When we arrived at the house, I decided I would try to keep a low profile. I planned to say as little as possible, smile when spoken to, and get through the long weekend.

As it turned out, Ryan had distant relatives in Vegas who invited us to their house on Christmas Eve for drinks and catching up. With my own family, when someone brings a new face to a gathering, that person can expect to be pulled into conversations and joked with as if they've been around for years. My family is really good at making people feel welcomed—we are communal people. When I found out that I would be meeting more people in Ryan's family, it made me nervous. I thought I would be in the spotlight as the newcomer. Those fears turned out to be unfounded; I was not only *not* regarded as someone to get to know, but I wasn't spoken to the entire night by this branch of the family except for the introductory "hello." I couldn't be too upset. While it was surprising to be completely ignored, this made it easy to isolate myself and blend into the background just as I'd intended.

After a while, I found myself sitting with the matriarch, who had obviously thrown back a few too many drinks. We hadn't had many interactions prior to this. She had been portrayed to me as a little "crazy" and outspoken, the one who bought into conspiracy theories and was best ignored. They neglected, at the time, to tell me she was an alcoholic. There we sat, me avoiding her gaze and watching the clock, when she decided to break the silence. The matriarch leaned in close.

"Sooooo, tell me," she slurred. The strong stench of alcohol on her breath made me recoil as she asked her burning question: "Is Obama a good Black?"

The woman hadn't spoken more than a handful of phrases to me the whole day that we'd been together, and this is what she chose to say to me? Why was she asking me this? How could she not see how inappropriate this was?

Clearly this woman was drunk. As I would learn over the years, there would be plenty more vitriol to spew and more alcohol to help it flow out of her mouth with ease. That Christmas Eve, as I squinted my eyes at her in disbelief, she didn't catch the hint that I was not going to participate in this conversation. My mouth was open, but no sound came out. She continued, "Are your parents good Repub—oh, it doesn't matter."

Realizing at this point that she might try to engage me in a political dialogue, I started feverishly giving my husband our secret signal that means "Let's get the hell out of here!" He spotted my SOS after a couple of minutes, and soon after that we were out the door.

"I was glad to see you giving the signal," Ryan said on the drive home. "I was kind of getting tired myself."

"Yeah, it's been a long day," I replied quietly. I didn't want to talk about it. I just wanted to go to bed.

For Christmas Day, Jewel invited her paralegal to dinner because she had no local family and would otherwise have spent the holiday alone. Imagine my surprise and pure joy when the door opened and on the other side was a Latina woman! For one afternoon, I was not going to be alone! But at the same time, I was nervous for her. The Jenn of today would have immediately gone up to her to warn her about what she was walking into, if not telling her to leave altogether.

Or better yet, the Jenn of today would have broken the silence by standing up and interrupting the problematic comments that would eventually be directed toward this poor, unknowing woman. But the Jenn of 2010 was still in shock over the things that had been said so far that weekend and was naïve enough to think that the presence of a stranger would keep everyone on their best behavior, sparing me from any more ignorant comments about race or culture.

Things started off fine as the food was prepared. Everyone was busy doing their own thing. Then we all sat down at a large table and started eating. It wasn't like a typical gathering of eight adults where you might have various little side conversations going on. No, it was a conversation led by the matriarch in which everyone sat silently as she grilled our new visitor: "So, where are you from?"

"I was born in Honduras."

"I've been to Spain a few times," my mother-in-law proudly chimed in. What that had to do with anything, I'll never know.

Ryan's grandma continued, "You speak good English."

"Well, I moved here when I was young, so I grew up speaking both languages."

"Good. Because we like people that speak English."

It was at this point that I pushed my chair back from the table and stormed into the kitchen. I was done with dinner, and quite frankly, I was done with every last person at that table (minus the paralegal). Ryan, his sister, and his mom all speak Spanish. His family spent years as a host family to students from Spain, and his mom even took off for weeks to immerse herself in the language because she knew how important it was to know more than one language. I was sitting with people who knew the value of bilingualism and were silent in the face of the matriarch.

We like people that speak English. I'll never get that phrase out of my head.

Every job I've ever held has called on me to use Spanish, my second language. My various jobs and friendships have allowed me to be in close proximity with the Latinx community, and to say that I've fallen in love with the language and the diverse cultures that speak Spanish is an understatement. I've seen firsthand the ugliness of "English-only" campaigns and the attempts by English speakers in the U.S. to shame and guilt people into giving up their home languages. I firmly stand against those views, yet there I was, in the presence of someone who was unapologetically expressing those very attitudes that I objected to. And no one said a thing. Not even me.

Unlike the silence I had chosen for the sake of harmony in those early times with Ryan's family, this silence was different. This time I was making a silent retreat to seek refuge within myself. I was afraid. I was afraid of what this all meant for what my life would look like in this family. I was still very much a newlywed, still trying to figure out my place in this new family with whom I'd previously had relatively little contact. I was discovering, much to my dismay, that I didn't have a place at all. And Ryan wasn't lifting a finger to create a safe space for me. I'm not even sure he recognized that I felt unsafe, which was even scarier. He was unable to recognize the prejudice and racism that was so clear to me.

Christmas dinner was just another example that contributed to the mounting evidence that I'd married into a family that generally held values and beliefs that ran counter to my own. It foreshadowed how alone I was going to feel in the sea of family members that didn't, couldn't, and had no desire to see things from my perspective as a person of color. I was horrified that not a single soul at the table recognized how isolating that exchange must have been for our visitor.

No one did or said anything to counteract what was being said. It was apathy, at best. At worst, the silence was their tacit approval of Ryan's grandma's opinions.

What appeared to be a thoughtful gesture (inviting this woman to Christmas dinner because she had no family in town) turned out to be an act of carelessness that made her a sacrificial lamb brought to slaughter and laid across a table of judgment and apathy.

The physical act of removing myself from the table was enough to catch my husband's eye. He soon followed me to the kitchen. "Are you all right?"

"I'm done with dinner."

"What's wrong? What happened?"

"I can't. I just can't. We can talk about it tonight."

At that point, I was livid at what I had witnessed all weekend, scared by their implications, and desperate to be back home. If I had talked about it in that moment, I would have burst into tears. Underlying all my feelings was the deep, agonizing sting that the person who knew me most profoundly didn't demonstrate any recognition of what I was experiencing. I was silent for the rest of the day.

On the off chance that our Christmas visitor is somehow reading these words and recognizes herself as the person who had the misfortune of coming to dinner that day, I want you to know that I saw you. I heard what was being said. I have replayed that afternoon in my head more times than I can count and my heart aches because I was not in a position of emotional strength to speak up for you and to let everyone around that table know that I did not stand with the views that were expressed. I lament it most because I know it gave you the impression that you were alone. You were not alone. I hope you can understand that my shock and pain prohibited me from speaking up for you, for myself, for anyone. It doesn't take away what happened, nor does it make it OK. Just know that I saw you, that I continue to think about you and your experience that afternoon, and that I am really, really sorry that I couldn't be an ally in that instant. It will always be a moment that fills my heart with deep regret. You were not alone. I am so incredibly sorry.

It takes more than love to shake the shock

For years, I beat myself up over my inability to speak out against all of the problematic and harmful things I heard Ryan's family say in that one weekend alone. Now, looking back, I have learned to give that girl grace. I wasn't silent out of apathy. I was silent out of fear and shock. I'd started becoming familiar with Ryan's family's cultural ignorance, but what I witnessed that particular weekend was completely unanticipated.

I'll be honest. If that weekend with Ryan's family had happened prior to getting married, it would have ended our relationship. No doubt about it. But that wasn't the case. We were married, and I didn't see any option of walking away. At the same time, I knew that all the love I had for Ryan (which was so, so much) was not going to overpower and cancel out the hurt and panic I felt at seeing who his family was.

When Ryan came and asked me to explain what was wrong, it was important that I was able to recognize that the kitchen was neither the time nor place. There was too much to unpack, too much to process. I didn't want to cause a scene and fulfill the stereotype of the angry Black woman. Was it OK for me to be angry? Absolutely. But when someone's actions cause me to lose dominion over my own emotions and responses, I've lost. And after all I had seen and heard that weekend, I refused to lose to them.

Chapter 4

The Trauma That Lies Within

Ryan and I climbed into bed that night, but we didn't lie down. We sat opposite each other—Ryan with his legs crossed, me with my knees pulled tightly into my chest. The lights were off, but the glow from the streetlight outside the window illuminated the room just enough for us to see one another.

We looked each other in the eye without saying a word. I, for one, was nervous to have this conversation that I knew was coming whether I wanted it to or not. Thankfully, Ryan started.

"What happened today, babe?"

My heart sank. My head was swimming. It felt like every ounce of air had been squeezed from my body. My eyes welled up with tears and pleaded with him to take those words back. How did he not see it? How did he not see any of it? In that moment it became clear to me that, even though we had spent it together, we had experienced very different weekends. Why weren't the comments at dinner troubling to him? Why didn't he say anything in the car on the way home from the airport? Didn't he see what was happening? Didn't he *see*? Yet here I was looking into the eyes of my husband, and the only thing I saw staring back at me were his eyes searching mine for some sort of explanation. I was devastated. I thought what sent me out of the dining room that afternoon should have been painfully obvious.

As the words poured from my mouth faster than I could clearly enunciate them, I began to sob uncontrollably.

"This whole weekend has been terrible! This has been the worst Christmas ever! I just want to go home!"

Silence.

"Did you hear your grandma at dinner? We like people who speak English?! What was that all about? Why didn't anyone say anything? That poor girl!"

Silence.

"Your grandma is the worst! She asked me last night if Obama was a good Black! What am I supposed to say to that? What does that even mean? What counts as a good Black? What's a bad Black? Why would she ask me that? I would *never* ask her if someone is a good white!"

Silence.

"And your brother and sister! They sat in that car and picked apart my features to figure out what country my family comes from! Who *does* that? You were there and you said nothing! Why didn't you say anything?"

I think Ryan knew that he was supposed to offer me comfort, so he took me in an embrace, but it felt empty. It lacked the warmth that comes from someone who truly understands.

I didn't sleep well that night because of all of my racing thoughts. *How did this happen? How could I be with a man who didn't recognize racism and prejudice in his own family? Why was he not outraged? Was he going to address this with his family? What does this mean for the future when we have children? Who is going to protect them? Who is going to protect me?*

Though our courtship and engagement were relatively short and primarily spent thousands of miles apart, I knew Ryan well enough to know that he didn't hold racist values. It was during this weekend that it crossed my mind for the first time that he didn't have the skill set needed to advocate for me. I didn't know what was holding him back, but I sure knew that loving me wasn't compelling enough for him to step into action. That's what hurt the most. I felt unsafe with his family, and he was not able or willing (I wasn't sure which) to step up to the plate and protect me. I was also learning that my shock was preventing me from protecting myself. All I could do was withdraw into myself and suffer in silence as people looked at my aloofness and wondered, "What's wrong with *her?*"

At the time, I was not able to put into words what I was experiencing. All I knew was that the experiences I was having with Ryan's family touched a very deep and personal nerve. It hurt in a place that I couldn't describe and filled me with panic and fear. I just wanted to get away from them, but the only thing I could do was cry about it—simply break down and cry.

What I experienced with Ryan's family that weekend was only the tip of the iceberg. Not only did their comments and actions affect me emotionally in the moment, but without knowing it, they were activating emotions and reactions from previous experiences.

For all of my childhood and most of my adolescence, I had received plenty of prejudiced remarks from friends and acquaintances, and I hadn't known how to respond. Every time, it felt like a sucker punch to the gut. I was always surprised that someone I associated with felt the way they did, and I felt like a coward for not having the words to say something to interrupt the conversation.

It wasn't until I went to high school—the first time I was consistently in a space with a diverse mix of people—that I saw people speaking truth into harmful conversations. I saw people my age who were skilled at doing so because it had been cultivated in them, and they had been doing it for years. I was awestruck, and yearned to one day be strong enough to insert myself into a conversation to stop the flow of prejudice and racism.

A couple of years into college, my roommate, some of her friends, and I were in our living room. Ricky Martin came on the TV screen and one of her guy friends remarked, "That guy is such a fag."

I immediately turned toward him and said, "Whoa, we don't talk like that in this apartment."

"Well, he is." The guy laughed defensively while looking toward the others in the room for support. "He's a giant fag."

I stood my ground. "I don't tolerate that kind of speech."

"Fag, fag, fag, fag, fag."

The room got quiet and people shifted in their seats uncomfortably as they waited to see what would happen next.

I pointed to the door. "Get. Out."

"I'm not here with you, I'm here with her," he said, gesturing to one of my roommate's friends.

"Well, her name isn't on the lease. Mine is. And I want you gone. Goodbye."

He couldn't argue with that. My roommate wasn't going to argue with me. The guy got up and huffed and puffed his way out the door. I don't know if that was the best way to handle the situation, but it was a huge personal victory in using my voice. With satisfaction, I watched him leave and then turned my eyes back to the TV.

I was tired hearing of people's ignorance about marginalized groups. I was done. I took the attitude of "It's someone else's turn to deal with this." With practice (and I had lots of it), it became easy to drop acquaintances and friendships that required too much of my emotional bandwidth. Did I lose lots of opportunities to help others understand what I was going through? Certainly. Was it my responsibility to educate? Nope. Sometimes you just have to "exit stage right" from a relationship that is mentally taxing in order to achieve self-preservation. Period.

Preferring to take the path of least resistance in the case of toxic relationships, the idea that I could not so easily remove Ryan's family from my life was suffocating. It was devastating because I had taken such care to remove their type of aura from any of my intimate relationships. I was unprepared to have those kinds of attitudes back in my life in a potentially profound way. This wasn't just going to impact me; I immediately thought about what this would look like once Ryan and I had children. I thought back to the questions and comments I had endured as a child that opened my eyes to the fact that I was the "other."

"Is your whole family brown too?" (I know you were only five, Kelsie, but your question has stayed with me all these years. It's one of my earliest memories of being othered.)

"He's saying poop when he looks at you because you're the color of poop!" (It was confusing when your three-year-old cousin kept pointing at me and saying, "poop," but I was embarrassed when you explained it, Neal. I had a secret crush on you, and you were comparing me to feces.)

"Why do you all [Black people] have weird smelling hair?" (I don't even know why I tried to explain hair products to you, Melanie. It didn't make any difference. To you, it just "all smells bad.")

"Well at least my nose isn't like *this*!" (Really, Alec? It was a third-grade peer editing exercise. I was *supposed* to correct your spelling error. To this day, I still shake my head at how you chose to flatten your own nose with the palm of your hand and make that retort in response to being corrected by me.)

I still shudder when I think about those questions and comments. They make me so sad for the little girl who had to endure them. Of course, as an adult, I feel their weight more heavily because I understand the bigger system of racism and ignorance that they're part of. I recognize how those many, many comments cumulatively strip away at a child's ability to feel "normal" and experience a true sense of belonging. The reverse didn't exist. My white friends and their experiences were normalized. To know about society in general was to know about whiteness. It was not to know about me. Not **my** experiences. Not **my** family, **my** skin color, or **my** physical traits. These were all subject to questioning. What I saw as normal was unfamiliar to my peers, and it was never clearer to me than in those moments of questioning from people I called my friends.

The seeds of self-consciousness began to take root and sprout within, and I can remember these thoughts forming as early as five years old. Now, having witnessed Ryan's family's insensitivities to the experiences of others, I was fearful that they would be my future children's introduction to what it was like to be the "other." My family (nuclear and extended) was my safe space for me as a child. I'd never had to justify any part of my existence to them. In Vegas, I realized that my kids might not grow up with the same security, and that left me panic-stricken.

That Christmas experience gave me the extra burden of realizing that whatever my future looked like with this new family, I would be braving it alone. My husband enjoyed his time with his family and was unalarmed (or, even worse, unable to perceive) their ignorant and sometimes outright racist remarks.

Looking back after doing the work to heal from my racial trauma, it's clear that his family were triggering things from my past. But at that moment, I didn't even know that was something to be considered. I just knew that his family was no family I desired to be part of. That was really all I could express to Ryan in that moment. It felt stifling.

"I don't like your family. I can't be around them."

In the immediate aftermath, I kept the details of our Vegas trip a secret from everyone I knew for a lot of different reasons. No one else was going through this dynamic in their relationship (although, I now know that we are all so good at faking happiness). Plus, we were so young in our marriage. Married for just under two years, my immaturity compelled me to portray the picture of newlywed bliss lest we be labeled for certain failure. The progression of our relationship from dating to marriage was relatively quick, and I didn't want to become a cautionary tale for all of my unmarried friends.

So, I ended up feeling alone. Many times throughout my life, I had been made to feel alone. I often felt like the odd person out, as much as I tried to fit in. This time, of my own doing, I isolated myself and my struggle from everyone I loved.

Walking away from my relatively new marriage never crossed my mind. Instead, I racked my brain for past indications that I'd missed that would have hinted at my ending up in this situation. It caused me to replay conversations in my mind and analyze different exchanges, but I almost always came up empty.

I don't know if it was pride or naïveté, but I refused to believe that I had entered into a marriage that wouldn't last. Ryan and I had overcome the obstacles of a long-distance relationship; we had beaten the odds. This was another obstacle we would face, but I didn't see this as something that would end our marriage. Clearly, Ryan didn't have experience in recognizing and dealing with racism; but he cared about me. He loved me. If I just explained this to him, if I just showed him, he would get it.

Countless times, I've found myself being the lone Black person in the room, and therefore thrust into the undesirable position as the "representative of my race." Without asking for it, I was put in the role of the teacher. Any person who has been tokenized knows what this feels like. The weight is on our shoulders to show that we are non-threatening and relatable; and we are expected to indulge different questions about our experiences, our culture, our hair, our bodies, and anything else that falls outside of the mainstream as if we are otherworldly. It's essentially explaining one's own humanity. It was a role that I stopped playing years prior in college, but for the sake of my marriage, I would reprise the role of teacher and help my husband understand. At the time, I didn't realize how hard it would be for him to see this invisible monster called Racism.

The January following the Christmas from Hell was one of the toughest times in our early marriage. Ryan constantly walked on eggshells, not sure what would set me off, while I weepily moped around. Not a day went by that I didn't relive that horrible weekend in my mind. Not a day went by that I didn't beat myself up for staying silent in the face of what I experienced and witnessed. Every time, it produced more tears—tears of disappointment, tears of despair, tears of shame.

I cried because my husband was oblivious to what was going on.

Ryan tried to understand. Boy, did he try. "Can you tell me again what happened?" he would ask even though it felt like we'd been through it a hundred times before. I cried harder each time my tears were met with his confusion.

"Why do you let this affect you so much?" That one cut like a knife. As if I *chose* to be this miserable.

I cried for our unborn children who would be brought into this mess. I cried for the task I had ahead of me to not only fortify them against the racial ills they would face in society, but also in their own family. I cried because I felt alone in my marriage. I cried about it all. I wanted him to act. I begged him with any words I could think of to reach out to his parents.

"Call them and tell them what happened—tell them what your grandma said to me!" I pleaded with Ryan. I was convinced that if they just knew, his parents would be mortified by what their kids had said to me, what the matriarch asked me, and what their silence communicated to me during Christmas dinner.

"They need to make this right!" They would make it right. Wouldn't they? I was their new daughter, after all. Right?

Looking back on it now, it almost seems unfair that I would ask Ryan to talk to his parents about this. He was clearly incapable, and I don't mean that as an insult. I was asking him to do something that he was not equipped to do. He didn't understand me when I told him how I was feeling, yet I was asking him to convey my hurt to his parents. I shake my head at that now; but at the time, I didn't understand that, and all I could do was make lots of noise to signify that I was not OK—that I needed help.

Ryan, who had yet to go on his journey of transitioning to a properly functioning adult relationship with his parents, was reluctant to reach out to his mom and dad. He was still very much the eldest child who sought the happiness and approval of those who raised him. The conflict that resulted from that Christmas put him between a rock and a hard place. He felt pressured to please me, his wife, but that meant that he would have to say something displeasing to his parents. On top of that was the very real difficulty he was having in understanding why the weekend with his family hurt me so deeply.

"I can call them and tell them what happened, but I don't know how to help them understand why it was such a problem. I don't feel the pain you feel."

"Ryan, I don't understand. You see how hurt *I* am by this. *I* am your *wife*. You should be hurt and angry because *your wife* has been hurt. How come you are unaffected by my pain?"

"It's one of the rules I live by," he said matter-of-factly. "I never want another person to be capable of affecting my feelings so much."

I was indignant. "But we're married! Your feelings can't be unaffected by me!"

Ryan sighed. "I'm willing to talk to them. Can you just tell me again what happened? I'll take notes and make sure I tell them everything."

The most innocent result of white privilege is sheer blindness. For weeks, we had variations of this same conversation. For weeks, and for what ended up being years, I bore the burden of providing evidence of my pain to my husband while at the same time trying to protect myself. I couldn't understand why the sight of my pain wasn't reason enough for it to feel personal to him. I didn't understand why he was unable to drum up some empathy. I think Ryan thought it would eventually fizzle out, but I was too shaken. I was paralyzed by this painful event and unable to move past it or go an entire day without thinking about what implications it had for my existence in this family. Once Ryan realized this was going to be a perpetual source of conflict, he finally called his parents about two months after the Christmas from Hell. Though I wanted him to tell them everything about that weekend, he chose to address the comments his grandma had made.

"Oh, she's of that generation," his mom started. "You know how old people are. Don't pay any attention to her. We don't."

And that was that. They never reached out to me. Ryan never pushed the subject any further. In their minds, they had addressed it. The subject was closed. No one ever asked me if I had closure.

And that's how the cycle of trauma continues to have life.

It takes more than love to push back on unacceptable behavior

Too quickly people will point to a person's inability to stand up for themselves as an indication of low self-worth. That's too simple an assessment. I had always been a child with very high self-esteem, despite the subtle and not-so-subtle messages from society about what my worth was as a Black child. I received constant praise not only from my family, but also from the other amazing adults my parents brought into my life as my mentors. It was never about low self-esteem for me.

The problem for me was that I was afraid of the consequences of speaking up. When it came to peers, I was afraid of losing friendships (the currency of childhood). But more often than not, my offenders were adults who had authority over me, and I was always taught to respect adults. Whether it be a teacher, a coach, or a neighborhood parent, it was not clear to me that standing up for myself was acceptable and necessary no matter who I was pushing back against.

It wasn't a natural thing for me to do. My parents had never intended their teaching on respecting adults to imply that I had to put up with off-color jokes or discriminatory actions; but it also hadn't been explicitly taught to me that adults may do mean things and I was well within my rights to demand that it end. Thankfully, my time in high school showed me kids who were doing this and allowed me to hone my own skills.

Naming and confronting problematic behavior is a skill to be practiced. It is something to be taught and nurtured. Yes, there are some people who come by it quite naturally, but because I feel so deeply, I am susceptible to tripping over my words when my emotions run high. It is something I have to manage to this day, and something I am continually working on.

Chapter 5

True Reconciliation

A few weeks after Christmas, I got a call from Ryan's sister, Jewel. We had not spoken since Vegas, so I hadn't had the opportunity to tell her what kind of impression the whole experience had left on me. Staring at her name as the phone rang, I went back and forth about whether or not to answer. I hadn't had time to think about how I was going to move forward with Ryan's family. I was struggling to just move forward with my own husband. If he was grappling with understanding the hurt that I felt from that holiday weekend, I had very little faith that anyone else in his family would. Did I have the strength to be honest with her about what had happened and the part she played in it? I had two choices—either ignore the call or answer and let it all out. I didn't have the emotional capacity to pretend there were no hurt feelings.

I picked up the phone deciding to see where the conversation led us, not knowing what I would say.

"Hey," I answered timidly. "What's up?"

"Hey," Jewel answered. "Do you have a minute?"

As it turned out, I didn't have the opportunity to say much at all—my sister-in-law dove straight into an apology. Her voice a little shaky, she pushed through her discomfort and embarrassment to get the words out. She began to recount what the weeks following Christmas had been like for her.

Once our time together was over and we had all gone back to our homes, her roommate returned to the house. They started swapping stories about the different things that had happened during the holidays. Not anticipating any sort of negative reaction, Jewel talked about the car ride home in which she used my physical features to attempt to pinpoint my country of origin. She recapped the cringeworthy conversation at Christmas dinner in which her grandma affirmed her appreciation for those who speak English.

Jewel's roommate didn't hail from Fargo. Coincidently enough, she was from Omaha like me. Though white herself, she grew up in a context far more diverse than my sister-in-law and was immediately able to objectively view the events of the weekend. She was horrified. Not one for being silent, she explicitly pointed out each indignity and didn't hold back. She explained how and why that weekend must have been hell for me. That was a turning point for Jewel that eventually led to her calling me.

I remember less of the words and more of the feelings from that conversation. I remember hearing tears on the other end of the call—tears of sadness, tears of shame, tears of humility, tears begging for forgiveness, tears that moved me to shed tears of my own. I remember a promise to do better, to be better, and to stand by my side. She was going to take up the burden as much as she could and fight with me.

"I want to be your ride or die."

Teary and snotty, I let out a laugh. "Ride or dies for life."

And like that, we were bonded. Rather than a sister-in-law, she felt more like a sister. I felt deep gratitude for our conversation. I felt a hopefulness that had previously been lost as a result of Ryan's inability to understand my point of view. I felt relieved that I was no longer alone in a family where it was painfully obvious that I "wasn't in Kansas anymore."

The apology was powerful. It wasn't artificial; it was from the heart, and I felt it. She wasn't sorry for the way it made her look—she was sorry for the way it made me feel. She could have easily leaned into a presumption of innocence by virtue of ignorance. She could have easily deflected what her roommate sought to teach her by claiming that it wasn't her intent to make me feel small, objectified, and alone. But she didn't do any of that. She didn't hide behind her ignorance. She owned up to the role she played in my experience that weekend without a shred of defensiveness. She saw that she was out of her league when it came to recognizing these situations and took on a posture of learning. She listened. She heard. She believed. She repented.

I could accept her apology because of this. It was clear that she understood what the hurt was and how she'd contributed to it. It didn't mean she would never hurt me again, but I could trust that she would try like hell not to. Her new awareness of the hurts I felt that weekend taught her the importance of seeing things from a different perspective than her own. It taught me a lot about a person's ability to yield to humility.

I think back to that call from Ryan's sister as one of the most memorable interactions I have ever had. In a world that is wrought with disingenuous and performative apologies, the humility shown during the call that day is what we would all hope to receive once it has been brought to a person's attention that they wronged us. Jewel's awareness of prejudice and racism in the world was not complete after that one conversation with her roommate. She would continue to develop a clearer understanding and grow in her allyship and anti-racism for years to come (as I hope we all will). But in that moment, she knew that she had contributed to a wound, and she chose to do her best to tend to it.

Her apology made the response from Ryan's parents all the more confounding and hurtful. They weren't trying to see things from my perspective. They didn't understand the hurt and had made the decision that it wasn't worth their time to investigate how that Christmas weekend could have impacted me in the way that it did. In years to come, they would double down on their resistance to seeing situations through any other lens but their own.

It was humbling to watch Jewel as she began to view her family and past experiences with a perspective and context outside of the one she had grown up with. It was not a fun journey for her. She was confronted with some harsh realizations about the people she had grown up loving the most. But once you wake up to certain truths, you can't unsee them. If she ever had regrets about choosing the path of awareness, she never expressed them to me. She went full steam ahead in her support and never turned back.

I owe a debt of gratitude to her amazing roommate. If you're reading this, you most certainly know who you are. Thank you. Thank you for speaking up on my behalf at a time when I was desperate for a lifeline, but hopeless, not knowing where one would come from. Your ability to identify and speak up about the horrors that you empathetically imagined I had experienced changed the whole trajectory of our family. You could not have possibly known the impact it was going to have. I certainly didn't. Because my relationship with Jewel was restored, we were able to move forward and develop a strong friendship and true sisterhood. It was because of this closeness that only a few months later, she flew to Chicago to tell me in person that she was gay and that you two were more than just roommates. This was huge, as she wouldn't come out to the rest of her family for years.

We became outsiders together, and our bond only became stronger. Though it ultimately didn't work out for the two of you, you will always have a special place in my heart because of what you did for me when I couldn't do it for myself. Thank you. A million times over, thank you.

Jewel, over the years your voice has grown stronger, louder, and bolder—not just for me, but for yourself. I'm on your side and forever in your corner. Thank you for being an example of how to repair what's been broken. Thank you for showing me the power that true forgiveness can have on both people. Thank you for getting in the fight when it would have been much easier to just stay out of it. Thank you for speaking up to the bullies in our "shamily" when I was too broken and bruised to do it. Thank you . . . for all the stuff. Every. Single. Thing. Thank you.

To the broken and bruised Jenn, the survivor of the Christmas from Hell: Thank you for picking up the phone that day. Thank you for not using your pain and anger as justification to cut off a person who would grow into a co-conspirator. Good for you.

It takes more than love to achieve reconciliation

Reconciliation is a direct result of the actions taken by one person to mend a wound they have caused. It isn't accidental and is only achieved through an earnest effort to earn the trust of the person they have hurt. I know there are some wounded people who just need space and time for healing to occur, but I needed an explicit apology. I needed someone to name the hurt they had caused and to own up to it. Too many times people give half-hearted apologies without really taking a deep look at the pain they have caused. And because they don't do the work to understand their error, they keep on causing pain. For me to move on, I need to know that *you know* what you did.

That's what I got that day with Ryan's (my) sister. That conversation is proof that reconciliation is real, truly attainable, freeing, and healing. It gave me such hope. In moments of hurt, I had assumed I only had two choices: pretend I was fine for their sake or cut them off for mine. That day, I learned that major hurts like this didn't have to end a relationship. There is such a thing as moving forward. Relief washed over me. Her resolve to work on her own awareness in order to show up for me left me grateful. I wouldn't have to pretend or tiptoe around her. She was safe. There really was a path to reconciliation.

Chapter 6

The Cycle of Stress and Tension

At the beginning of our marriage, Ryan and I established an easily agreed upon tradition of alternating between our two families for Christmas. Three years in, we had our first baby and moved to Omaha to be close to my family. It then became an option to spend time with my side of the family during the holidays *and* see Ryan's family, either by driving to see them or hosting them in our home.

After the Christmas from Hell, my mind and body began to go through what would become a perpetual cycle of stress and tension that revolved around seeing Ryan's family during the winter holidays. It generally began in September, when his mom started talking about December plans, and lasted through February, when I finally regained some of my sense of self.

No matter how short the time with Ryan's family was (and believe me, I always tried to make it as short as possible), I was sure to hear or see something unpleasant. It never failed. So yes, I stressed out once Ryan's mom started alluding to spending the holidays together.

Each year, the mere mention of seeing his family incited a panic within me. My head started swimming. It became hard for me to concentrate. My body language shifted as I crossed my arms and avoided eye contact. Irritability was high. Sometimes I'd get weepy. My expressions of not wanting to see them came out in a variety of ways:

"I don't want to see them."

"Can we not?"

"I can't think about that right now."

"How many days?"

"I don't like being with them."

"They're not kind."

"We have different views."

Each year, from September until Christmas, I would be in a perpetual state of agitation in anticipation of seeing Ryan's family. I'd play different scenarios in my head (some hypothetical, others that had happened before) and come up with a response so that I wouldn't be caught off guard.

OK, if his dad tells my daughter again that her natural hair is crazy, I'm going to step in front of him, look my daughter in the eyes, and say, "Your hair is not crazy. Your curls are beautiful."

When I was satisfied with the response I came up with, I moved on to the next potentially damaging remark and came up with a rebuttal for that.

If his mom makes a disparaging comment about Jewel and her wife for being gay, I'm going to interrupt the comment and say, "We love the tías (Spanish for "aunts"), and you're so lucky to have two aunts who love you very much."

My months of preparation were a futile exercise. I stressed myself out thinking up different hypothetical scenarios to combat, only to have something completely out of left field catch me off guard. When we traveled up north, I felt like a fish out of water in a cold and unwelcoming home with people who felt like anything but family. Yes, I had found an ally in Ryan's sister, but her schedule didn't always allow for her to fly home and join us for the holidays. And after her marriage to another woman, her relationship with her parents became estranged and she wasn't present for family gatherings at all.

As someone who has been othered her whole life, I'm acutely aware of disparaging comments toward any marginalized group. Repeated comments, even those made in jest, allow for the dehumanization of people and the absence of empathy. It was and still is my goal to speak up when I'm in the presence of remarks that permit someone to look at another as less than. That's why, when I heard something inappropriate during my time with Ryan's family, I felt shame for not having the courage to say anything—not only to the person who said something inappropriate, but to the entire group of people who sat by and didn't flinch at what was said.

Like the time Ryan's dad—in reaction to hearing about someone of the Jewish faith—became shifty-eyed, adopted a sinister grin, clasped his hands together, and said, "Hmmm, much profit!" Everyone else laughed at his impression playing on the anti-Semitic trope of Jewish greed. I was mortified. As the years passed, the feeling of being the only one in the room who saw things differently became a usual occurrence. I no longer looked for recognition in the eyes of my own husband, whose longtime proximity to this behavior made it as natural as the air he breathed.

Unintentionally, I became a skeletal version of myself whenever I was around Ryan's family. I responded to any questions with short, one-word answers accompanied by a fake half smile. I tried to avoid interactions altogether. I had been burned too many times by truthfully answering a question or letting my guard down and showing my personality. The slightest hint of vulnerability was met with a scoff, an unknowing stare, or sometimes a complete change of subject without any acknowledgment of what I had said.

At other times, I was just stunned into silence—like the time Cousin Wayne stood in the middle of extended family wailing, "Did you know that in just a few years we, the white race, are going to be the minority? There's something wrong with that!"

Cheeks burning, the only brown person in the whole group, I had no words for that. I looked over at Ryan to see how Wayne's statement sat with him. If he had any negative feelings about it, his face showed no signs of it. Oh, but Jewel to the rescue.

I leaned over and whispered to her, "So he doesn't want to be a minority because he knows minorities get the short end of the stick?"

Without missing a beat, Jewel turned the attention on to herself. "So, Wayne, you don't want to be a minority because you know minorities are mistreated in this country. Is that it?"

As my kids would say, "Ohhh, sick burn." Thanks, Jewel—you sure took the wind out of his sails as he sheepishly got off his soap box. That was satisfying.

It wasn't just what I would hear that stressed me out. Only steps away from where Ryan's parents proudly displayed pictures of my kids, they also prominently displayed their Confederate flag magnet (how someone from North Dakota feels an affinity to the Confederacy, I'll never understand). The first time I saw it on the fridge, I just avoided its hostile gaze. It mocked me with its red, white, and blue colors that were supposed to stand for virtuous attributes while still somehow justifying keeping people like me enslaved.

I pointed at the magnet with disgust and asked Ryan, "Why do your parents have anything with the Confederate flag on it in their house?"

Ryan stopped what he was doing with a puzzled look on his face, as though the thought had never crossed his mind. "Oh, um, I don't know."

"Well, it's super offensive," I said. "You know what the Confederacy stood for, right? It's racist."

"I don't think my parents mean anything by it. It probably just reminds them of the car from The Dukes of Hazzard. That's what it makes me think of," he responded.

Riiiiiggghhht. Ryan never actually asked them about it or responded to the fact that it was discomforting to me to see the flag, knowing its true significance.

The second time I went up to Fargo and saw this flag on the fridge, I took advantage of a moment of isolation and slid the magnet from its prominent position on the freezer door to the side next to the wall where there was just enough space for my hand to push it all the way to the back, far from my sight, but still eerily close to my consciousness.

The third time I went up to Fargo, I was shocked to find it had reclaimed its distinguished place of honor, front and center on the freezer door. Fed up, I found another opportunity of seclusion to snatch that magnet and put it where it should have been all along. I lifted the lid of the kitchen trash can, meticulously picked up scraps of rubbish and buried it. So long, you symbol of oppression! It seems petty, but it was my little act of resistance.

The fourth time I went up to Fargo, I was aghast to see that damn flag magnet back on the fridge. Did they go digging for it? Or worse, was it so important to them that they took the time and effort to replace it? Either way, just like in much of the South, this flag wouldn't die.

When our children entered the picture, my cold and distant demeanor gave way to a hyper-vigilance that sought to shield them from the ignorance arising from this family's lack of cultural awareness. I'd be damned if I was going to let my kids pick up phrases or mannerisms that diminished the existence of another person. Since I couldn't trust myself not to freeze up, I was ready to usher them out of a room at a moment's notice or raise my voice level when talking to them so as to drown out a nearby conversation that I didn't want them to hear.

Consequently, I could never just be in the moment and enjoy my kids when Ryan's family was around. I tried to straddle both sides of the fence, playing with the kids while being on high alert. Even something as simple as playing with toy cars became a complicated task.

"Vroom vroom, Mommy!" My son giggled with a monster truck in each hand.

I moved the truck in my hand back and forth on the ground. "VROOM!" I roared loudly.

This earned a happy laugh from my son and he drove his trucks in circles on the floor where we were sitting. "Mommy, can your truck do this?" Silence.

"Mommy. Moooommy. Moooooooooomy. MOMMY!"

My head whipped around. "Yes! What? What is it?"

"Mommy, you weren't listening to me."

No, I wasn't. I was trying to listen closely to a nearby conversation Ryan's mom was having on the phone to make sure it was safe for us to be around. I will always regret those years that I allowed Ryan's family's presence to zap the joy from the interactions I had with my own kids.

I grew up with all four of my grandparents and have always valued the bonds of those special relationships. In the short-term interests of my children (and perhaps due to some wishful thinking), I decided to not stand in the way of them developing a relationship with Ryan's parents. I hoped that, through loving these brown children, their eyes would be opened to the harm of their flippant indulgence in stereotypes. Maybe Ryan's dad's need to over-accentuate accents when repeating the words of someone from another culture would cease. Maybe they'd both understand that they didn't need to give cultural descriptors, like "this Black guy" or "the Bhutanese man" or "this Mexican woman," in every story they told. But the only thing that changed with the passage of time was my growing anxiety as I became aware that my kids were becoming more interested in the conversations going on around them. By the time my oldest was five, I shifted from wishful thinking to wanting to protect my babies' minds and hearts. I was preoccupied with guarding their emotional safety and warding off the potentially damaging effects on my kids' concept of the world around them. It eventually grew into wanting to stay away from this branch of the family tree altogether.

I knew the only way Ryan would consider eliminating their presence from our life was if his parents were doing the children physical harm, which they weren't. It wasn't even worth the conversation or argument. He still didn't understand how his family contributed to my pain; there was no way he would go for keeping his parents' grandchildren from them.

I called the time after we'd spent a Christmas with Ryan's family my "detox period." It was the time it took for my mind and body to relax again after being on heightened alert for the months leading up to Christmas and the actual time spent with his family. The detox was never just a gradual release of tension. There were days when the tension would decline, but then I would torture myself by replaying comments or situations in my head, and I would get tense all over again. For all the mental prep I had done beforehand, those exact situations never came to pass. I could think of a hundred different snide remarks that might get made, and sure enough, they'd say something that hadn't even crossed my mind. I'd get caught off guard and shocked into silence—again. Then I'd get angry at myself for not having anticipated the comment or situation beforehand.

I loved being with my husband; the problem was that I did not love being with his family, and years of this dynamic began to create troubles for Ryan and me.

There were plenty of arguments with Ryan during my detox period because I was angry at his inaction. He became defensive and told me he couldn't do anything about a situation he didn't witness. Or if he *did* hear the same comments I'd heard, he took no offense at them, which I couldn't understand. It was a constant reminder that I was alone in my struggle. I was alone in my pain. I was alone on this journey of navigating these dynamics. It's my firm belief that he would have stepped up to say something in the face of overtly racist comments. But even then, only if they came from someone other than the matriarch. The whole family held her to a lower standard of social niceties and allowed her to go unchecked.

Because Ryan didn't do well at maintaining contact with his parents (especially in those early years), I could go months without having to hear from or about them in the wake of our time together. With them at a safe distance, I could start to relax. The Jenn my husband knew was able to re-emerge after a few weeks of being kind to myself—indulging in binging my favorite shows, going to bed early, or losing myself in a book. By February I was in a recovery of sorts and able to connect with Ryan once again. It would remain that way until the following September (if we didn't have to see them at any other time).

When I think about this now, it's maddening that I tortured myself in this way. But I didn't see it like that back then, and I still sometimes veer into this mode of thinking that I can prepare myself for whatever may come my way. At the time, the mental anguish I would put myself through was worth the idea of being able show up in the moment and demonstrate to my kids that we must always say something to interrupt the flow of ignorance. But it literally consumed my thoughts, day and night.

Years later I realized that, because of this vicious cycle, I was usually spending a good four months of my life every year with my mind and body in stress mode.

Four months.

One third of the year.

Roughly 120 days.

And that's only if we saw them once in a calendar year.

It takes more than love for the body to release the emotional pain it retains

Imagine walking down the street, minding your own business, when out of nowhere a snowball hits you in the back. The first time, you're caught off guard, curious as to who threw it and why, but you shake it off as a one-time thing. Then, without warning, another snowball comes from another direction. This time, more forceful. You encounter a smiling oncoming walker who suddenly launches a snowball in your face. The mental whiplash is blinding—you did not expect that from someone who *appeared* friendly. You're on guard as another person approaches and you hold your breath wondering if you'll be hit again. You breathe a sigh of relief as you stay to the right and pass that fellow pedestrian without incident, only to be pummeled five seconds later with two snowballs from the left.

By this time, you've been hit with so many unexpected snowballs that you're constantly on guard for the next one to come. You can't anticipate when, from what direction, or from whom. They'll have varying degrees of impact; some will be packed with ice or, even worse, be snow-covered rocks. Anyone who comes your way could be a person who's going to throw one at you, but there's no way to know with certainty—no one is safe until they've proven themselves as such.

This is the best way I know how to describe what I have felt, at times, merely living my life as a Black woman in the U.S. While warranted, it's extremely unhealthy to maintain this level of stressful vigilance, and anyone who walks around carrying this weight is the one who suffers. With work, I've gotten to a place where I don't live in this vigilance constantly, but there are certainly environments that put me right back in that headspace.

It has been said that our bodies hold onto our emotional scars and that it comes out in a number of ways. I lost sleep and carried a lot of tension in my shoulders. Ryan, who likes to give neck and shoulder massages, would often come up behind me and comment on how tight my shoulders were. I wonder if he ever equated his parents' visit with what he was feeling in my muscles.

The stress of being around them did not melt away as soon as they were out of my presence. I wish it were that easy. Because I felt like them coming into my home or us going to North Dakota was something Ryan brought upon me, my body not only had to relax from having them nearby, but also had to learn to let down the walls I had up against Ryan, who I felt was choosing his own desires over my best interest.

That negative tension didn't just go away on its own. I had to fight to reclaim myself every single time. This pattern seared itself into my existence for a decade, intensifying with each passing year of compounding microaggressions and unresolved hurt. To make it even worse, I was still shouldering the brunt of this burden in silence. When asked by family and friends about Ryan's family, the most I would reveal is that they could sometimes be "culturally ignorant". I let them jump to their own conclusions about what that meant. I never fully went into to detail about what I was experiencing, not even with my parents—especially not with my parents

They came of age during the Civil Rights era. My mom was a member of the first integrated class to graduate her high school. My parents have stories of their own battles fought—life under Jim Crow and overtly racist practices to keep people like them out of certain spaces. They worked hard so that I could have a different experience. And while they certainly achieved that, I felt like it would break their hearts to hear what it was really like for me when I spent time with Ryan's family.

Chapter 7

Therapy, Take One

"Babe," I said, turning toward Ryan, "I think I want to start going to therapy."

The cycle of stress and tension had eventually become too much for me to manage on my own. Truthfully, I wasn't managing it. I was just surviving. After four years and two kids, I made the decision to try therapy.

"Yeah?" he said. "I think that's a great idea."

That was still to be determined. I was hesitant about interacting with the therapy community because Ryan was a therapist, our last name is not common, and all the local therapists seemed to be familiar with one another. I had a lot of nagging questions that, up until that point, had kept me from pursuing help for myself.

"Do you need my help with finding someone?" he asked.

No way—there was no way I could go to someone who knew Ryan. *Will they be able to give me unbiased feedback? Can I be open about my struggles with Ryan and his family without it reflecting poorly on him? Will he lose credibility in working with marriages and families if people find out his own family is having problems?* I wondered.

Ultimately, my own self-care won out. I shook my head. "No, I want to do this on my own."

"OK, babe. Sounds good. I'm happy you're doing this."

I knew about a website for looking up local therapists. The site had different filters to help people find a good fit. I didn't have any names of people or practices to start from, so I used these filters to guide my search.

I don't think I care about the gender. I'll leave that unchecked.

Faith? Yeah, I think I'd like someone with a Christian foundation. I'll check that.

Someone who specializes in marital counseling would be good. This is affecting my marriage after all. Check.

I guess that's good enough?

I hit the search button, and my heart immediately sank as the results popped up on the screen. The therapists were all white. And at the top of that list? Ryan.

My Ryan.

For a moment, I almost decided to end the search right there. My fears shifted from someone possibly knowing Ryan to walking into a room and pouring my heart out to someone who couldn't relate because they were white. It reminded me of the one pre-marital therapy session we'd had during one of my visits to see him in Tennessee. We didn't have a lot of money at the time, so we found a therapy student (someone Ryan didn't know) who was willing to see us at a reduced rate. She was young, white, and thought it was appropriate to start our session off by smiling at me and saying, "I have Black friends." I should have turned around and walked right out, but against my better judgment, I stayed.

The budding therapist folded her hands in her lap and leaned forward. "So tell me, what are some of y'all's concerns going into marriage?"

I took the lead in getting the conversation rolling. "I'm concerned about privacy issues. I'm a lot more private than Ryan. He's like an open book, and I'm not. I'm nervous he won't be able to discern what's okay to share with other people and what's not when it comes to us."

The young therapist-in-training pursed her lips together and slowly nodded. "Yep, in my classes we've talked about how this dynamic can exist in couples of different races."

I furrowed my brow in confusion. I didn't mention anything about race. An awkward silence ensued.

"Um, yeah," I started. "I just don't want him airing all of our dirty laundry."

"Yes!" She nodded feverishly. "That's the exact phrase they used in the textbook!" She looked pleased and continued after a pause. "Are you at all concerned about the race thing?"

Ryan wasn't jumping in with anything to say. This was becoming a conversation between the student-therapist and myself.

"I mean, it's no big deal for my family. And Ryan has assured me that it's not an issue in his family. I am a little concerned that his dad's first comment when he saw my picture was 'nice tan.'"

She cocked her head to the side and looked at me as if I were the one missing something. "Well, you are pretty dark."

I didn't say much for the rest of the session.

I tried to shake that memory out of my head and looked again at the search results. I reminded myself that my experience with that therapist-in-training was not indicative of what I would experience this time around. I skipped over Ryan's name and scrolled through the thumbnail photos, clicking on any that seemed warm and inviting. After opening several tabs, I browsed through the descriptions and eventually landed on a woman whose picture and brief bio gave me the impression that she was understanding and caring. She looked to be around the same age as my mom and had years of experience under her belt. I decided to go with her and give this a shot. I was desperate. I needed to try something. Anything.

Walking into that first therapy session, I was like a gambler walking into the casino without any extra cash to spare. I went in with an emotional deficit, hoping to hit it big with this potential connection. But if I lost, I was sunk. I had a lot riding on this, and I needed it to work. To hit the jackpot, I had to put in all my chips; I couldn't hold back at this first meeting. I laid all my vulnerability at this stranger's feet because I needed to know sooner rather than later if it was going to work. I started at the very beginning of my relationship with Ryan and went through all of the experiences, all of the comments, and all of the feelings.

It was both amazing and alarming how I could remember every single slight and the emotion that accompanied it as I retold it to this stranger. That moment was the first time that I had verbalized the entirety of what I was experiencing in one sitting. I didn't always have the words to describe it; what I couldn't put into words, I made up for in tears. By the end I was sobbing and exhausted. Had she offered me the chance to take a nap, I could have curled up into a ball right there on her couch and fallen asleep.

Having told her all that I felt she needed to know, I sank into myself—bringing my knees up to my chest and resting my head on them. I was nervous for her reaction. This was it. This was the moment that would tell me whether or not I had found someone I could move forward with. This was the moment when I would learn whether or not this stranger would become my therapist.

"Wow. It's clear that you have been deeply hurt by Ryan's family, and it sounds like he has not taken responsibility for setting appropriate boundaries to keep you from getting hurt."

I let her words sink in for a moment before I spoke. This was the first time I had looked at it as a boundaries issue.

She continued. "It sounds like you are needing Ryan to stand in the gap for you—to take on the comments and hurtful actions from his family instead of leaving you alone to bear the brunt of those things."

I nodded. "Yes. I do feel like Ryan puts it all on me to figure out how to coexist with his family."

"Do you ever tell Ryan this?"

"When it gets really bad, I have no choice but to say something. But a lot of the time, I just keep it inside. I don't know what to say to get him to understand what I am feeling. I'm tired of having the same conversations, the same arguments. I don't want to fight with him. I'm afraid I'll say something that I can't take back."

"So you've lost your voice with your husband?"

That was a new revelation to me. "Yeah, I guess I have."

Even though I had made it clear that my being the only person of color in my new family was the source of a lot of grief, what stood out most to her from my story was that I wasn't fully communicating with Ryan and that Ryan wasn't stepping up to address boundary violations on the part of his family. We were going in a different direction than I had anticipated, but it seemed valid. Whether it was fighting ignorant remarks or his mom inserting her opinions where they weren't welcome, I supposed it could all be described as boundary issues. I'd wanted someone to get outraged on my behalf so that I knew I wasn't being overly sensitive, but I was desperate to have some sort of road map to help life with Ryan's family be more bearable. It was a relief to have something tangible to work on. Pushing any hesitation I felt to the side, I decided to move forward.

During our sessions over the next couple of years, I learned the importance of getting specific with Ryan when making my needs and requests known. My therapist and I had set a goal to communicate better with him about his family. But although we were coming up with solutions, we weren't talking about the root cause of my grief. We never touched on the *why*. We never delved into *why* I was so stunted in my capacity to talk to Ryan about how I felt around his family. We never delved into *why* I couldn't move on from the hurtful experiences I had with them. We never delved into *why* I continued re-experiencing the original emotions surrounding those initial incidents as if they were happening to me all over again. We never questioned if it was healthy for me to be around his family. The goal was to make my time with my in-laws tolerable.

With her help, I found words to describe my pain and to tell Ryan what boundaries I needed in place for me to be able to spend time with his family.

"No, I don't want to be in North Dakota for that long. The trip needs to be shorter."

I was learning to confidently push back on the plans that they made with no consideration for what Ryan and I might have going on.

"No, that's not a good time for them to come. They need to find another weekend."

When Ryan accommodated my requests, I felt heard. I felt seen. I felt loved. My needs were being acknowledged and tended to. There were still times, though, when I knew that what I needed in order to feel like my kids and I were safe directly contradicted his desires.

"Ryan, your parents are coming next week, but I see that you're still seeing clients."

"Well, yeah," he answered nonchalantly. "I don't want to take off more time from work than I have to."

"So you'll say, 'Hi,' and then you're going to leave me here with them by myself?"

"It's no big deal. They'll just want to play with the grandkids."

Though I had made strides in speaking up for myself in anticipation of an uncomfortable situation, any pushback I got had me retreating into silence. Fearing an argument, I chose to feign harmony in the marriage at the expense of my own peace. Obviously, I still had some headway to make in truly advocating for myself.

One nugget of wisdom from my therapist that I latched onto was that time with Ryan's family didn't mean my life had to be put on hold. I could still run errands and make plans. Little trips out of the house gave me the temporary reprieve I needed to recharge my batteries periodically during their visits. Target became my home away from home; their Dollar Spot drew me in and consumed at least the first thirty minutes of my visit. That freedom to spend as much or as little time as I wanted in each aisle was everything.

To support my personal therapy goals, Ryan and I even had a couple of joint sessions. We identified boundaries that were not to be crossed, and we discussed how Ryan would handle it if and when they were violated. Ryan could logically understand why it would be a good practice to lay down some of these boundaries, but he didn't feel like *he* needed them in place to coexist with his parents. Their behaviors didn't bother him. This meant that when he approached his parents with these boundaries, he was doing it on my behalf. He was just trying to please his wife while still making his parents happy, so he spoke to them in the most avoidant and non-confrontational way possible.

"Could you guys maybe ask us about potential dates before you decide when you're coming? We love having you, but we want to make sure that we don't already have other plans. It would just help us plan better, you know?"

"Mom, we just want you to be able to be Grandma. We don't want you to come and feel like you have to make up new rules for our kids.

Let us take that on. I know you're just trying to help, and I appreciate it. But we can handle the discipline."

It was one thing to agree these boundaries in the therapy room, but it was quite another thing for Ryan to implement them. Because he struggled to command respect from his parents, they initially bull-dozed right over them. They still came when they wanted and they continued to overstep and parent our kids. That aggravated me, and I let Ryan know every time. To his credit, he stuck with it and continued to tell them the boundaries they needed to respect. He turned up the heat one notch. When they told us when they were going to drop in for a visit, he started to say no. He told them those dates would not work; they'd have to find another time. This shed some light for us on how to have some success in setting boundaries—now instead of us being inconvenienced, they were the ones being inconvenienced. His parents started to hear him. It wasn't without griping, but they eventually did start to abide by some of the boundaries he was setting.

While I appreciated Ryan's efforts, these boundaries were set to nip the typical in-law annoyances in the bud, thereby making it more "comfortable" for me to be in the presence of his parents. Though he was trying to give me relief, nothing was addressing what it felt like for me to be around his prejudiced family. No boundary was set that addressed the permissiveness of racism in their home. No boundary was set that helped me feel like the racial identities of my kids and I were safe in their presence.

In the absence of those conversations, we were still in a situation where Ryan didn't show up in the way that my heart ached for him to. No opportunity was made for growth or healing on that level. I accepted that I could be happy that his parents would now ask us when a good time to visit was instead of just telling us what dates to put on our calendar. I could relax, a little, knowing my babies weren't subject to another set of parental figures every time we saw them; but that relief was fleeting. None of the boundaries put in place changed the fact that I had open emotional wounds at the hands of this family that only got bigger each time we got together. No one acknowledged my hurt.

Then one summer, shortly before our third child's first birthday, I finally got the courage to take a bold step. Ryan wanted to take a trip up to see his parents. As he started proposing dates to me, I bit my lip and shyly asked, "What if I didn't come this time?"

"Not come to Fargo?"

"Yeah. I could stay home with the baby and you can go up there and have a good time with the two big kids."

Ryan thought about that for a moment. "Hmm. That would make things a lot less stressful for everyone. It seems like a win-win situation."

And with that, a new normal was set. Ryan had a nice long weekend up in Fargo, and I ended up taking my daughter to Chicago to meet up with some friends. I didn't know it at the time, but that summer of 2016 would mark the end of my trips to Fargo.

As his own therapy practice grew, Ryan eventually found himself in need of a new office space. As it turned out, an opportunity opened up for him to share a space with my therapist. That was just a little too close to home for me.

"Really?" I asked incredulously. "You have to move into *that* office? You can't find another space?"

"The rent is way better than at my old place. And the location right off the interstate makes it ideal." He looked at me apologetically. "This doesn't mean you have to stop seeing her."

But that's exactly what that meant to me. Ryan tried to convince me that there was no conflict of interest, that I could continue to have sessions there. But I wasn't swayed. It was too uncomfortable to have him working alongside the woman I'd confide in about my struggles with him and his family. I felt like, once again, my emotional health was taking a backseat to what Ryan wanted. Shortly after he made his decision, my therapist and I had our last session.

She smiled at me. "I'm really proud of the progress you have made in the time we've worked together."

"Thanks. I feel like I am getting better at telling Ryan what I need, and I will continue to work on not losing my voice around him."

"I'm really rooting for you, and I hope things can get resolved. If it were me, I would be devastated if a rift in a relationship kept me from seeing my grandchildren as much as I wanted to."

In that moment it dawned on me that, for this whole time, I had been doing work with a woman who could empathize more with those who were hurting me than she could with me, her client. I had been seeing her monthly for about two and a half years, and in all that time, I don't know how I'd missed that. This is not to say that you can't go to a therapist who doesn't share your race, gender, heritage language, sexuality, or any other deeply personal marker that identifies you with a particular group.

I will say, however, that it has made me aware that therapists, no matter how well trained, are still human. Humans identify with other humans, some more closely than others. Humans have biases and limitations to their understanding of other people's experiences that are different from their own. *Could this be why we didn't tackle the race issue in therapy? Did she feel ill-equipped?* I'll never know. Having that light bulb moment made me more comfortable with the fact that our professional relationship was coming to an end. It served its purpose, and I could be grateful for that.

It takes more than love to find the right kind of help

My time in therapy was not in vain, nor was it without its rewards. It was only toward the end of the relationship that I realized that I was attempting to heal something that the person helping me wasn't prepared to help me heal. I'll never know if my therapist was avoiding the effects of race on the troubled relationships with Ryan's family or if she really didn't see it at all. What I do know is that this episode in my life taught me to seek out the best help for myself. In everything. If I needed someone to come alongside me in something, I needed to do my research and keep searching until I found the right person. When it comes to the important things, it is okay to reject the notion of "taking what you can get."

Chapter 8

Struggling to Understand

Back when I was still visiting Fargo, Ryan's grandma continued to make little comments to me about the Black race. She was adept at finding a time when she could lean over to me, out of the earshot of everyone else, and whisper one of her little "nuggets" of knowledge.

One year as we were visiting during Thanksgiving, she leaned over to me and said, "You know, the Blacks and the Indians have an extra gene that makes them alcoholics."

I stared at her, deadpan. Then I turned away from her to catch a glimpse of the faces seated around the kitchen table. Their continuous chatter indicated to me that no one had heard a thing.

"Did you know that?" Grandma pressed on.

I turned back toward her. "No, I wasn't aware of that. I'm not sure that's a real thing."

"Oh, it is," she insisted.

At this point, I had three options. One—I could cause a stink right then and there. I didn't want to do that. Two—I could just keep it myself like I had done so many times before. I already knew where that would get me. There was no benefit to doing that. Three—I could speak up and not stay silent, but I would do it on my terms. I waited until later, after the kids had gone to bed. I was nervous, but

I confronted Ryan's parents with the comments made at the dinner table.

"Today she told me that Black people and Native Americans have an extra gene that makes us all alcoholics."

Ryan's dad guffawed at that. "Really? Where does she come up with that?"

It wasn't more than thirty minutes later when I heard him in the other room on the phone with his sister. "And listen to what Mom said to Jenn!" His laughter continued.

Mentioning what she'd said earlier that afternoon was useless if its only purpose was as a source of comic relief. No one saw that I wasn't sharing in the laughter. Awareness wasn't the singular problem. It was awareness, insight, self-reflection—the whole kit and caboodle.

In anticipation of the upcoming winter holiday season shortly after her genetics lesson, Ryan wanted to have a phone conversation with his grandma to try to set some boundaries and hopefully spare me from her nonsense. His plan was to call and ask her to stay away from certain topics when she was in my presence, mainly race and politics.

"Grandma, do you think that's something you could do?"

Clearly not, because she got angry with Ryan and made it clear that she would be fine if she never saw me again. She wouldn't let him get a response in. Oh no, she had to have the last word.

"I feel sorry for you, I really do. I feel sorry for you for being married to her. She's a spoiled brat!" And with that, she hung up on him.

Though a bit surprised by her actions, I was actually relieved that she expressed not wanting to see me anymore. At least she felt the same way that I felt about her, and I wouldn't have to pretend I wasn't offended by nearly everything about her. If anything, I was more hurt by Ryan's laid-back attitude as he told me about his grandma's contempt for me as if he were talking about something as commonplace as the weather. But this almost certainly guaranteed that I wouldn't have to see her this Christmas—or ever again.

Just to be sure, I addressed this with Ryan. "I mean, you can't expect me to spend my holidays with her."

"No," he said. "I know."

"If we're going to see your parents, we need to set some major boundaries. And your grandma cannot be invited to anything we are part of. She doesn't want to see me; I don't want to see her."

He agreed. "It's for the best."

Though still unable to fully grasp the depths of what I was struggling with, Ryan was now at least ready to attempt to act on my behalf. Any grievance he expressed was always on my behalf because he was unfazed by the behavior of his family that he had become accustomed to over the course of his life.

He arranged a Skype call with his parents and the two of us to talk about our new conditions for spending time in Fargo. It would be the first time in a long time that I wouldn't just be a figure moving around in the background in one of their calls. Nope. Not this time. This time I was up close and personal.

The call started with nervous smiles from Ryan and his parents, while I sat, expressionless, looking off to the side. They skirted around the issue at hand with meaningless chitchat about the weather and local goings-on up in Fargo. Every so often I would look in the direction of the screen. When they had tapped that well dry, when it became more awkward to sidestep the conversation rather than to actually have it, Ryan started in.

"So Mom, Dad, we need to talk about what Christmas is going to look like this year. I had a conversation with Grandma, and she's made it clear that she doesn't want to see Jenn. And Jenn feels the same way. So if we are going to come up, it needs to be when she isn't there."

"Yeah, that seems like a good idea," his dad agreed, seemingly un-surprised by what Ryan had just said.

"Grandma was really nasty. She called Jenn names, and she hung up on me. I've never heard her be that mean before."

His mom got a look of sympathy on her face. "Honey, I'm sorry you had to see her like that. We never wanted you to see her that way, but she can be really nasty."

Did I hear that correctly? Are they apologizing to Ryan?

And that was that. Having gotten that conversation out of the way, they moved on to other more comfortable topics. I was never addressed at any point. But there was a silver lining. It wasn't all bad. It had been agreed upon that Ryan's grandma wouldn't be around whenever we went to visit. For that, and only that, I could breathe a sigh of relief.

That Christmas, we packed up the kids and drove up north to Fargo. It used to be an uneventful six-hour trip, but with kids in tow and bathroom stops aplenty, it was a crawl to the finish by the time we pulled into town. All I wanted to do was unload the sleeping children and collapse into bed. Kids in one arm and luggage pulled by the other, we dragged ourselves up to the door and knocked. We heard footsteps shuffle to the door before it opened.

The look of surprise on Ryan's face quickly turned to warmth.

"Grandma!"

"Hi, Ryan! Oh, you've got some tired kiddos! Well, come in and put them to bed."

I looked at Ryan, who returned my death glare with a sheepish smile. His grandma shuffled away from the door and returned to her spot on the couch.

"Ryan, I thought we all agreed that she'd be gone by the time we got here!" I snapped in a hushed but firm whisper.

"Yeah, babe, I know. I didn't think she'd be here. But it's getting late. She'll be going to sleep soon and then she'll probably go home in the morning. Besides, it's kind of good to see the old bird."

I had been duped. Ryan's parents had misled us so that they could see their son and grandchildren. It felt dishonest, and in that moment, I hated them for it. They chose to do what was more convenient for them rather than to keep a promise they had made only weeks prior. Ryan embraced the surprise. He never called them on it.

The old bird had a lot of eccentricities. Subscribing to just about every conspiracy theory there was, she refused to undress in front of the TV because "they're always watching." Ryan's family poked fun at her "crazy ways," but failed to make a distinction between her more benign unconventionalities and other characteristics that could have an impact on people. Her racist and prejudiced ways didn't impact them, so it was all one and the same. Odd was odd.

But for me, there was a clear distinction. Some of what they referred to as her "crazy ways" were actually racist, plain and simple. Ryan's family failed to realize that by shrugging off Grandma as "no big deal," they sent the message to me that her racism was okay with them. They didn't realize that she was just as much a representative of their family as any other member, and the fact that her racism was going unchecked was teaching me that they tolerated (or maybe agreed with) her racist beliefs.

Ryan wasn't raised with or taught to have empathy. His family had a very individualistic worldview: You alone are responsible for your experiences. No one else's actions have a bearing on your existence.

Since the entirety of our dating relationship was long distance, we didn't have the opportunity to confront racism together as a couple. We talked about it but were only able to speak in hypotheticals. Ryan's message was always the same: "I'll protect you."

The Jenn of today would push further and dig deeper during those conversations. At the same time, the Jenn of today may have made different relationship choices based on Ryan's responses, and that would have changed the whole course our relationship and our lives.

At the time, I failed to realize that Ryan didn't understand the beast that is racism. He was proclaiming to be able to protect me from something that he had never personally experienced. He couldn't begin to imagine what that would look like, what it would require of him, or how it would eventually play out when the perpetrators were people he had loved for his entire life.

In the beginning, I had every confidence in the world that Ryan could do what he had said: he would protect me. He hadn't given me a reason to doubt his abilities as far as I could see. With each passing incident that required my nudging and still resulted in failure, my confidence in him to stand up to the prejudice and racism in his family shrank incrementally until it no longer existed.

One of the qualities that I loved about Ryan was the same one that caused him to struggle when it came to recognizing and confronting racism. Since he held himself to the standard of judging everyone on their individual merit, he found it difficult to accept that other people didn't do the same. He saw racism as the result of one individual choosing to discriminate against another and never linked it to anything societal. Systemic racism, in his mind, was long gone with the passage of the Civil Rights Act and had no reverberations in the present. And in conversations where he entertained the idea of systemic racism still existing, he asserted that it wasn't in his circles, and he played no part in perpetuating it. One thing he liked to say to me was, "North Dakota is so far removed from things going on everywhere else. We don't understand racism."

He almost said it with pride, like North Dakotans were above the fray.

"We don't understand racism."

He was implying with that statement that they didn't have skin in the racism game—neither as victims nor as perpetrators.

"We don't understand racism."

He couldn't see how that statement allowed them to fully participate in and benefit from a system constructed to keep marginalized people at a disadvantage without taking any responsibility.

"We don't understand racism." *You're right, babe. You don't.*

It takes more than love to understand the implications of not understanding

Plenty of white people can admit they are out of their element when discussing race and racial discrimination. They'll cite the fact that they didn't grow up around people of color or that they were taught to not see color. True as that may be, those statements become problematic when they are given as reasons to not engage in conversations on race and racial discrimination. The admission of not knowing a lot about these topics should lead to discontentment and a desire to know more. There should be no comfort in ignorance.

When Ryan would look at me and tell me that he and his family didn't understand racism, he thought he was only making a simple statement about himself. He couldn't see how, having chosen to love and marry a Black woman, his acceptance of his own ignorance would affect me. Not understanding racism was his crutch. He used it to give his family members a pass rather to take a hard look at them. His crutch, while used to hold up his loved ones, continually beat me down. While it seemingly didn't affect him, it made things miserable for me when I was faced with racialized situations in this unfamiliar family and couldn't turn to my husband for support, understanding, or protection.

Chapter 9

Where's the Disconnect?

Writing an entire book about the most difficult part of our marriage might make it seem like it was all miserable. That was not the case at all. I loved my life with Ryan. The struggles we had with his family were compartmentalized. We learned to not talk about his family when we didn't have to, and we usually didn't have to if we weren't dealing with the holiday season or the occasional summer road trip up north.

Race came up plenty in our relationship and the conversations were quite productive when it was not within the context of his family. It was not a topic we avoided. I didn't care that he was white. He didn't care that I was Black. When it didn't involve his family, I had no problem talking to him about my experiences as a Black woman or pointing out things that I thought were racialized when I saw them happening. He never questioned my judgment on those things. He recognized that he was coming to the table with far less experience in looking at situations with an acutely awareness of how race factored in. He came to those conversations as a learner. In fact, he was eager and grateful to have his attention called to things that previously flew right under his nose without him noticing. I can remember him coming home excited or even proud of himself for being able to pick up on a racialized situation.

"Hey, babe! Have you ever noticed how when people tell stories and the person isn't white, they have to say the race of the person? Like, even if their race has nothing to do with the story?"

"Yes, Ryan."

"Yeah," he said pensively. "I just noticed that today. That's so annoying."

He was glad he was gaining the ability to view things through a perspective that wasn't originally second nature to him. And while I sometimes rolled my eyes when he expressed it, I loved that he was so open and willing to learn. He never made anything I did seem foreign or exotic or weird.

On our wedding night, when it was time to go to sleep, I got out my satin bonnet and put it on my head. Ryan smiled. "What's that for?"

"It's my nighty cap. I wear it to protect my hair from breakage so it stays healthy."

He leaned in and gave me a kiss. "You look gorgeous."

He didn't make me feel self-conscious, and this was usually how it was when he encountered something I did or said that he didn't understand. His easy-going manner made it really effortless to explain little things to him here and there.

Sometimes our conversations were a bit more involved. I often talked about what I wanted life to be like for our future kids. I grew up in the predominantly white part of Omaha. Because of that, my parents were intentional about making sure that we had a connection with the Black community and culture. Every Sunday we drove twenty minutes to North Omaha to attend church. They had plenty of Black friends and coworkers who would regularly come by and visit. Our house frequently echoed with deep laughter and Smokey

Robinson or The Temptations playing on my dad's record player. Did I still have racial baggage? Yes. But I'm grateful they put such an effort into making sure that my only sources of knowledge about my own culture were not family members and the five o'clock news.

I stressed with Ryan the importance of elevating Black culture with our kids. "I want them to learn about the rich cultural heritage of Black people because that won't be taught to them in school. I want to make sure they are proud of being Black too."

I got no pushback from Ryan. "Oh yeah, babe. I can totally get behind that."

I knew what it was like to grow up only seeing people who looked like me depicted in the history books shackled in chains or pummeled by the forceful flow of water from firehoses. And Ryan was able to acknowledge that he was taught only a minimal amount of history from the Black perspective.

"I need them to know the heroes, the heroines, the innovators, the artists, and the activists that shaped our culture," I'd tell him.

"Yeah, I get that. We won't have to lift a finger to make sure their whiteness will be affirmed."

We talked about having "the talk" with any sons we'd potentially have in the future. The talk his parents never had to give him. The talk his brother never received, but my brothers did.

"Don't play your music too loudly. If you get pulled over, keep your hands on the steering wheel. Just answer the cop's questions respectfully. Don't talk back. Make sure you don't move unless you're told to, and even then, announce your every move before you make it."

He just nodded. He knew what I was saying was true.

Ryan was nothing but affirming of my Blackness and how I chose to incorporate Black culture into my life. If I wanted to adorn our walls with Black art, fill our bookshelves with literature by Black authors, or accessorize myself with African-inspired prints, I was never met with anything but love. I was completely supported in all of my choices.

So where was the disconnect? How could my husband be so encouraging, so supportive of Black culture, and display an ever-growing awareness of inequities and disparities when with me, but be so aloof and seemingly unaware when it came to everything I was experiencing with his family? What was going on? At times, I felt like he was gaslighting me—his apparent inability to see these things with his own family sometimes caused me to question whether or not I was seeing and hearing what I was clearly seeing and hearing. Ryan and I would regularly talk about the ridiculous things that white people say to people of color. We'd roll our eyes and sigh at how ignorant some people could be. But when his family would say something similar in nature, that guy with the growing awareness was nowhere to be found. Ryan didn't even flinch.

It obviously felt isolating in the moment. You know when you hear something that causes you to raise your eyebrows? You're wondering if you're the only one who heard it? You start to think you're crazy, but before you reach that point, you meet eyes with someone whose eyebrows are touching heaven just like yours and realize, "Phew, it's not just me." That's what I wanted with Ryan on so many occasions but didn't find. Jewel had committed to stand by my side in the face of her family's ignorance, but she wasn't my spouse. She hadn't promised at an altar in front of all our family and friends to honor and cherish me. And she wasn't always in North Dakota when we were; her visits went from being infrequent to nonexistent as she went through her own battle of acceptance with her family over being gay.

While Ryan's silence had many consequences, there was one long-lasting impact that was the most devastating. Each time Ryan tried to reason with me about something a family member had said instead of getting upset on my behalf, I questioned how important I was to my husband. This was another way in which I felt like I was experiencing gaslighting—the two realities just didn't match up.

Ryan is super romantic. He is the guy who will send flowers just because, surprise me with gifts for no reason, and give hugs and kisses whenever I'm within arm's reach. His words never fail him; he is always complimentary and easily able to articulate how much I mean to him. He has always worked so hard to make me feel secure in his love; but when it came to what I viewed as the simple act of putting an end to the comments, questions, and off-color remarks, he couldn't (or wouldn't?) do that.

I was left feeling confused, frustrated, unappreciated, ignored, and unimportant. When those feelings crept into my heart, my mind took over watering all the seeds of doubt. I started telling myself that he only loved me when it was easy and convenient, but when it came down to it, his priority was and would always be to please his parents. I couldn't help but see a direct correlation between his inability to advocate for me and how he actually felt for me. I would argue this point with him.

"If you really loved me the way you claim to, you wouldn't subject me to this. You wouldn't have any problem confronting your family when they say and do these things!"

Accusations like those really pierced his heart. "I don't know what to say," he said exasperatingly one time. "My goal every day is to make sure you feel loved. This hurts so much because if there is one thing you question about me, I would hope that it wouldn't be my love for you."

We were two very hurt people in those moments, and we were stuck.

It took me years to realize that I was coming up against the powerful bonds of family and the dynamics between parents and their children. It was something I could relate to. There's something about walking through the door of your childhood home that wipes out ten to fifteen years of emotional maturity. Even now, as a mother of four children, it still happens to me. Unless I'm called to play referee in an argument, I'm basking in the glow of my parents' presence. There's a comfort from home that will always remain unmatched, no matter how far and wide I venture.

Will my parents ever just be adults to me? Probably not. I will always hear their words and watch their actions through the lens of being their child. They get the benefit of the doubt from me if they ever say or do something that causes me to cock my head to the side in confusion. I have so many loving memories of them that counteract any questionable thing they may have said or done in the moment. I still push back on a comment or an action, but my assessment of their character isn't reduced to that single incident. I would instead view it as a lapse in judgment.

Well, Ryan was experiencing the same thing. It wasn't that he didn't hear or see what his family members were saying and doing. It was that this was his family. These were the people who he'd always known to be loving. These were the people who had nurtured and cared for him and his siblings in the best way they knew how. These were the people who, as a child, he'd seen as superheroes. He was still looking at them through those eyes. If his dad made a disparaging remark about a certain group of people, he knew his dad didn't mean any harm by it. It wasn't an indication of who he was deep down.

This nostalgic lens—and we are all susceptible to it—can cloud our ability to recognize harmful behavior in the people we love the most. Even when I could point to a specific thing they had said or done,

Ryan would reach into his knowledge bank of who he knew them to be and give them the benefit of the doubt. I saw him do that often, like the first time I met his mom's mom. She didn't come around as often Ryan's paternal grandma, the star of the Christmas from Hell.

"The only thing the Muslims want is to kill Americans."

I looked around waiting for someone else to be offended by that comment. That moment never came. I spoke to Ryan later about it.

"Did you hear what she said about Muslims, Ryan?" I asked. "That's not true at all! That was so offensive!"

"I know, but that's just how she is. She is crass and misinformed, but she is one of the most generous people I know. Sometimes we have to yell at her because she gives away more than she can afford!"

If no one else saw this as problematic, what was I to do? More concerned about not rocking the boat in a new relationship, I opted for silence. The Jenn of today would never have allowed Ryan's response to be the end of the conversation. The Jenn of today would have pushed back. The Jenn of today would have asked Ryan why he was fine being okay with his family's brash and crass behavior. But I wasn't that Jenn back then, and so I didn't do any of those things. Instead, I stayed silent during those early interactions with his family and felt immensely out of place. And while Ryan let those moments come and go without incident, those same moments were the very ones that informed me about who these people were and what they were all about. And it twisted my stomach into knots.

Ryan saw my struggles with his family as me not liking them. It was so much more than that. I found their views and attitudes toward minority communities harmful. I didn't feel safe with them. Was I fearful that someone was going to physically harm me? No. But I couldn't relax in their presence knowing that I might be put in a position where I was made to feel inferior. That's what Ryan didn't get. He didn't understand that I was viewing them as a toxic presence. I pinpointed it from the moment I met them and, almost immediately, I started voicing the boundaries I wanted with his family.

"When we start having kids, this is going to be a problem."

"I don't want to raise our kids around your family."

"Living in Fargo is never an option."

Every experience around his family was stressful because I was always on high alert for whatever comment was going to come my way. When we had kids, my sole mission was to shield them from the ignorance of Ryan's family and give them the freedom to enjoy the time they spent with their North Dakotan side. I tried as hard as possible to never leave them alone in a room with his parents or any other extended family. Anytime someone started with ignorant speech, I distracted them or picked them up and moved rooms. I didn't feel like keeping my kids away from his family was a real option because Ryan wouldn't understand why it wasn't a positive thing for the kids to be around them. To even broach the subject would have been to cause more grief, and wouldn't have resulted in what I wanted anyway.

The fact that Ryan didn't understand all that was going through my head and what I was experiencing only added to my stress. My husband's emotions were more deeply connected to his own family than to me or my pain. What I was going through was not personal to him. I came off as someone pushing back on the image of who he knew his family to be. In his mind, I was the one who had it all wrong. I was the one who unnecessarily took things to heart and took his family seriously when I shouldn't have. For a long time, he defended his image of his family members and hoped things would get better over time. He hoped this was a question of acclimating myself to my new family.

He had no clue how deeply this was affecting me. My husband. The therapist. The Marriage and Family Therapist. This man whom I loved. He just couldn't see it through my eyes.

The goal was never to change Ryan's family, though it would have been nice if they'd made a radical change in thought and behavior. Most of his family wasn't hurting me on purpose, and I knew that. Spending the majority of their lives in a place where they were surrounded mainly by those who looked and thought like them, they had the freedom to speak and believe as they pleased without any impetus to self-reflect. My entrance into their family was not about to change that. Having lived in a place so devoid of people of color, they were unable to see in real time the effects that prejudice and racism had on the targets themselves. They were unable to hear and see these things the way I heard and saw them.

Ryan grew up in a community where people could make insensitive jokes and subscribe to racist ideologies without people challenging their thoughts. Anyone who questioned them was shrugged off as not understanding them. None of them would ever self-label as being prejudiced or showing bias, but that's what a lot of their speech revealed. They considered themselves nice, hardworking Christians who loved everybody. They became defensive if anyone suggested that they demonstrated otherwise. The disconnect was real.

No, my goal was never to change these people. My only hope, what I longed for, what I desperately needed, was for Ryan to wake up to my reality with his family. I needed shielding. I needed protection. I got neither.

It takes more than love to see someone you love from another person's perspective

The people we love, even at their worst, get the benefit of the doubt. We know that they are more than that one hurtful thing they said or did. The people we love have deposited so many happy experiences into our emotional banks that a little withdrawal here and there in the form of negative interactions doesn't amount to much. That was Ryan. His cup was overflowing; his emotional bank was full. His family and how they operated was all he knew; and he had turned out to be a happy and healthy guy, so how bad could they be? But then I came into the family. I came, opened a brand-new account, and they started making withdrawals almost immediately. Ryan tried to float me a loan.

"My grandma would give the shirt off her back to anyone who needed it."

"That probably didn't come out the best, but he really has a good heart."

For those wanting to rush to the quick defense of friends and family who mean well, it is extremely important not to. If someone you love has wronged a person, and that person has the courage to say something, listen.

Listen, because an outsider's perspective is valuable.

Listen, because you may learn something about the people with whom you surround yourself.

Listen, because it may shine a light on growth areas in your own life.

Listen, because it may introduce a different way of thinking, speaking, or acting that is more productive.

Listen, because your happy memories don't cancel out someone's negative experience.

Chapter 10

Finally, It Has a Name

My journey to understanding the deeper, underlying causes that were amplifying my issues with Ryan's family took some time. It started with a hint that I kept in the back of my mind until it was confirmed and pushed me to get the real help I needed. It came at a time when I least expected it, in the last place I would expect to find it.

Just on the heels of my two years in therapy, I was working as a bilingual liaison for a local high school. There were many miscellaneous tasks associated with my job, but the part that I found most rewarding was assisting immigrant families in learning to navigate services in the community (think the school system, DMV, the bank, the postal service, etc.).

I heard a variety of different stories of how families came to the U.S. Each story was unique and deeply moving, with every imaginable emotion interwoven in the narrative. Since I'm fluent in Spanish, I was often asked to interpret in meetings or translate documents. Too many times to count, I heard disparaging comments from teachers about their students' inability to perform in class.

"He just sits there like he is bored, but he's got lots of missing assignments. He has plenty to do."

"I find it really disrespectful when she won't make eye contact with me."

They misinterpreted a student's disinterest in class as being disrespectful without knowing what a student was dealing with outside of the walls of the school. I tried to explain these things, but I also recognized that I was not the best person to articulate the students' experiences in a way that would resonate with the teaching staff. Luckily, my work had put me into contact with plenty of people far more in tune with the experiences surrounding immigration, and I knew the perfect person to address our staff.

I reached out to my friend and asked her to come and speak at one of our staff meetings. Her presentation provided a wealth of knowledge, starting with broad definitions and eventually focusing on the challenges that our particular group of students were likely to face.

"Trauma can occur as an emotional shock from a stressful event or physical injury. And for many of our students, immigration can be a traumatic experience," she said at one point.

Wow. I had never thought to associate this experience with trauma.

She continued, "Trauma is the closest thing we have to time travel. When a person's trauma is triggered, it is as if the initial trauma is happening all over again. Their body reacts in that moment the same way that it did back then."

My body began to tense up. *This resonates with me. This resonates with ME. Oh my gosh, I understand this!*

It was like a giant missing puzzle piece had just fallen into my lap. Yes! I understood exactly what she was talking about!

For years I had replayed the story of the Christmas from Hell and Ryan's parents' dismissiveness of it all in my mind, in therapy, and after some time, for a few chosen friends who I trusted would cheer me on. Every single time, I cried, my body got tense, and it took me time to calm down afterward.

Could my experiences that Christmas be trauma-related? I kept listening.

"Trauma is something that has to heal properly. Imagine you have a broken arm. If you don't receive the proper treatment, which is to put a cast on it, the bone will never fully heal as it should. It will heal itself the best way it knows how, but your arm won't have its full functionality. Trauma works in the same way."

I looked down at my lap as my eyes started to well up with tears. *I think this is me. I think she is talking about me. I get this.* Without knowing it, this woman was putting words to a pain that, up until then, I had been unable to describe.

This was why I couldn't properly repair the relationship with Ryan's parents yet had been able to have a fully trusting relationship with his sister. His parents' refusal to address my pain forced me to function the best way I knew how in their presence. Our relationship would always be dysfunctional so long as we avoided talking about the hurt and addressing it. Just as a broken bone doesn't heal correctly without the proper attention, so too does a relationship suffer without the proper care. On the other end of the spectrum, Jewel had taken the time to address the hurt and tend to the wound, so we were able to reconcile and have a fully functioning relationship.

But it went beyond my immediate struggles with the racism and prejudices I witnessed with Ryan's family. What she was describing also explained the effects of the cumulative emotional shocks I had received throughout my life. The shock of people's words and actions directed toward me. The ignorant questions, the exclusion, or the unnecessary highlighting of my differences—it's not something one ever becomes numb to, but something one learns to weather. It explained why I walk into a public place and count how many other people of color are present. It's why I change the way I talk in the presence of white people—void of slang of any nature. It's why I always ask for a bag and receipt even if I just buy a pack of gum—I don't dare walk out without a proof of purchase. According to what I was hearing, it was possible that I was walking around with Trauma Brain.

My mind started racing. *Wow, could this really be what's happening? Trauma? That's a BIG word. Maybe I'm overexaggerating a bit here?*

As if having heard the thoughts in my head, my friend continued speaking. "Immigration can leave our students and families with Post-Traumatic Stress Disorder (PTSD). When most people think of PTSD, they think of people who have gone off to war, but it can affect anyone who has suffered trauma."

I was one of those people who had thought trauma was exclusively related to war. I'll never forget what she said next. "A traumatizing event for one person may not be a big deal for the next person. Two people could have the exact same experience but internalize it in different ways. We may find ourselves surprised at the types of events that cause trauma in a person; and we also might be shocked that something isn't as traumatizing to someone as we would expect it to be."

No one gets to be the judge of my experiences.

Imagine being sick, but no one can tell you what's wrong. You can feel it in your bones—something is wrong. You spend countless hours visiting different specialists and Googling all of your symptoms, but no one can pinpoint the problem. If you've gone down that path before and have finally found someone who can give you an accurate diagnosis, you know the relief and gratitude that come with that discovery. Finally, there's a name for what you have. Finally, you can move forward on a path toward healing with confidence.

That's the relief I felt that day. That's the gratitude I had for being in that room at that very moment.

From that point on, I began looking back on the Christmas from Hell with new eyes. Things started making sense. It was no wonder I could only freeze up and cry when I talked, or even just thought, about it. No wonder I couldn't just get over it. Though each passing year placed it further and further into the past, it always felt as if it had happened only yesterday. As profound as this realization was, I kept my thoughts about having gone through a traumatic event at the hands of Ryan's family to myself, still a bit self-conscious about using such a big word to describe my experience. Armed with this knowledge about myself in relation to my in-laws, I was even more intentional about making sure that I took time away from the house during their visits.

The final piece of my puzzle wouldn't come until five years later, in 2019. By then, I had left my job as a bilingual liaison, gone back to school for an additional master's degree in elementary education, and was now a kindergarten teacher. The school year had recently started, and Ryan, the kids, and I were enjoying a visit from Jewel and her wife, Lucy, during the Labor Day weekend.

I sat down at my kitchen table with Lucy and she immediately wanted to know how I was feeling. Ryan and I were preparing to host his family for Christmas in our new home. While Lucy was going to skip the holiday with the entire family, it was the first time Jewel was going to participate—her own marriage had put a rift between her and her parents nearly three years prior.

How was I feeling? "I'm dreading it," I confessed. "I don't know how I agreed to this."

"I can see you tensing up just thinking about it," she observed.

"I have never built trust with them ever since the Christmas from Hell. Ryan told them how hurtful that was for me, and they just blew me off and explained it all away."

Lucy spoke with a slight hesitation. "I've always heard you refer to that Christmas, but do you feel like it's something you could walk me through?"

I was able to do so, but not without plenty of tears and pauses as I made my way through the story.

She looked at me. "You've been traumatized by them. Every time you see them, they are triggering your trauma."

"You really think so?"

"Oh, absolutely," she said.

I was immediately mentally transported back to the presentation I had heard five years prior that explained what trauma is, and I shared this with Lucy. "I heard someone talk about trauma years ago and felt like she was describing my situation, but I've been intimidated by labeling it with such a heavy word."

"Oh, no. You're dealing with trauma. You have unprocessed emotion when it comes to Ryan and his family's ignorance about racism and prejudice. This is trauma. This is racial trauma."

That was the first time I considered that I was experiencing racial trauma. The hurtful events that had affected me so deeply centered around Ryan's family's disregard for my experiences as a Black person in their space.

"Jenn, have you heard of EMDR?"

"No." I grabbed my phone to look it up. "EMDR. Eye Movement Desensitization and Reprocessing." I tried to skim the information to get a quick understanding of what I was looking at, but it was in vain. "What is this?"

"It's one of the treatments for PTSD. It can reduce the emotional distress that is tied to painful memories. I think you should look into finding a therapist specifically trained in EMDR who can help you with your racial trauma."

That conversation changed everything for me. It was the first time I became aware of a way out that didn't require something from Ryan's family that I knew I would never get. This was work that I could do, with guidance, which might release me from the emotional cycles that ensued when we saw his family. It was a lot to digest, but I was ready to take this step toward healing and, hopefully, closure.

In the weeks that followed that fateful Labor Day weekend conversation between Lucy and me, Ryan noticed that he was getting an increasing number of new clients whose marriages were heavily affected by trauma. Not knowledgeable in that area, he referred many of them to others to get the proper help they needed. This happened enough that it prompted him to recognize his need to expand his scope of practice, so he signed up to for a program to learn about trauma and become trained in administering Eye Movement Desensitization and Reprocessing, or EMDR.

One day after a training session, he came home, walked right past the kids, and took me in a long, tight embrace as he buried his face into the curve where my neck and shoulder meet.

"Hey, babe," I said, caught off guard. "Is everything OK?"

Nothing but deep breaths. *Is he crying?*

"Ryan? What's going on?"

He pulled back to look at me. "Today we talked about different types of trauma and what can trigger a person."

I looked down to avoid his gaze. "Oh."

"We went through all the signs of a person who's been triggered."

Silence.

He went on. "The more we talked about it, the more I realized that I see those signs in you. Jenn, I think you've been traumatized by my family. I feel so awful. Here I am, living with someone who is traumatized, and I never saw it."

I looked up at him, and our teary eyes met. "Yes."

It takes more than love to recognize deep pain

Sometimes the very last people to know that we are suffering are the ones closest to us. I don't know why that is. Optimism? Desperation? Avoidance? Lack of awareness? I really don't know. Whatever it is, our loved ones want to believe that we are okay. And they'll hold on to that belief until it's undeniable that we are not.

Many find it surprising that Ryan, the counselor, was unable to see how deeply I was affected by his family. I'm one of the lucky ones. My husband received training that opened his eyes to my pain, but the majority of people don't get that benefit. This is less about Ryan's inability to identify trauma and more about how easily trauma goes unrecognized in our society.

How many people's pain do we pass by and write off as something run-of-the-mill? Do we even see the pain? Trauma manifests itself in a number of different ways, and there are hurting people around us all of the time.

How many times do we take someone's silence as standoffish and rude?

How many times do we turn our noses up at someone who has had a public outburst about some seemingly small inconvenience?

How many times do we judge someone for being too sensitive?

Trauma can be as complicated for the untrained eye to spot as it can be to unpack all the ways that a traumatizing event has changed a person. We'd be better as a society if we all did our part to learn to recognize when our brothers and sisters are hurting so that we can meet their pain with compassion instead of judgment.

Chapter 11

A New Understanding

With fall changing to winter and the year inching to a close, our almost simultaneous revelations about racial trauma marked the beginning of what would be a long road of change for us—both as individuals and as a married couple. While I was grateful for this realization in our marriage, I had to fight the urge to think that, up until this point, Ryan hadn't been taking my concerns about his family seriously. But that hadn't been it at all. He had always taken me seriously; he just didn't have the context to understand the signs that I didn't even realize I was showing. I was stunted in my ability to communicate my pain to him, and he was ill-equipped to read between some very blurry lines.

It's more accurate to say that he had a new understanding of my feelings, reactions, and behaviors. Now, with the knowledge of what it meant to experience a traumatic event, he recognized that when I objected to spending time with his family or recounted hurtful experiences with them, this was not just me complaining about them. He finally understood that this was hurting me deep inside, in a way that I was unable to cope with. Now he better understood why every seemingly minor violation on the part of his family evoked a tremendous amount of emotion on my part.

Something that had always bothered him during our marriage was my tendency to shut down when conflict arose. He called it "going cold on him," while I referred to this side of myself as "The Ice Queen." Though dissociative identity disorder (previously multiple personality disorder) is a real mental health issue, that is not what I'm referring to here. The Ice Queen is the image I use to refer to the state I was in when Ryan and I dealt with conflict.

I never wanted her to show up, and I got mad at myself when she did. Did I have moments of immaturity that resulted in me giving Ryan the cold shoulder? Absolutely. But that's not what I'm talking about here. The Ice Queen was someone entirely different, making me unrecognizable even to myself. She generally showed up while planning a visit with my in-laws, after a visit with my in-laws, or in any discussion where I didn't feel supported by Ryan. I've come to realize that being blown off is a big trigger for me. That explained why, after all those years, I had an even greater emotional reaction to Ryan's parents' apathetic reaction to the Christmas from Hell than to the actual events of that Christmas.

From Ryan's perspective, he saw his wife emotionally shut down as The Ice Queen arrived. Void of any pleasant disposition, she went from being very talkative to barely saying anything at all. Eye contact ceased, and she physically drew away from him. If he and The Ice Queen were sitting together on the couch, her touch became cold and distant. If they were standing in the kitchen, she'd hug herself and turn her head away. He knew something was wrong but thought, *She's an adult. She knows I'm here if she wants to talk. I'm enabling her if I keep pursuing her.* So, he'd walk away. Though it hurt his feelings, he wouldn't allow himself to take it personally.

For me, however, it was a very different story. When I was "going cold on him," as Ryan would call it, I was retreating from a conversation that was causing me emotional distress. My eyes would dart from object to object within the room, looking for a place to anchor themselves without ever fully being satisfied. My mind raced with thoughts, most of which didn't have the strength to rise up from my throat and break past my lips. I knew Ryan wasn't aware of the internal conflict behind my silence, and it caused me such grief when he would insinuate that I was just choosing to stop talking to him.

He would ask me if I was okay. I would only respond with a silent nod even though my entire demeanor said the opposite. Inside, I was searching for the words to tell him what was bothering me. I always came up short.

The silence was deafening. My eyes would plead with his to just recognize the inner grief I was feeling, but I was always met with his concerned, yet confused, silence.

"It seems like you want to be alone. But I'm here if you want to talk."

Ryan would usually lean over and kiss me on the cheek before walking away, happily humming. Seemingly unaffected. Always unaffected. And I was left beating myself up about why I couldn't come up with the words to tell my husband what I was feeling.

After we gained awareness of trauma, and the role it was playing in my life and our marriage, we were able to recognize The Ice Queen for who she was. She was the meek, emotionally paralyzed version of myself, a compilation of my painful parts. She was the one who was hindered by pain, shocked into silence, and feeling alone. She was unable to find the words to make herself understood. Knowing who she was allowed Ryan and me to have more productive conversations about her.

"When The Ice Queen comes," he started, "I don't know what to do. I want to support you, but you don't talk to me, so I think you just want to be left alone."

"That's the last thing I want from you. I want you to stay. I *need* you to stay."

"You just want me to sit with you?" he asked.

I nodded emphatically. "I want to talk to you, but I'm afraid."

"What are you afraid of?"

"I'm afraid that I will unleash on you. I know the power of words. I don't want to say something that I can't take back."

In my most painful moments, the words that I wanted to speak to Ryan reflected those of a wounded soul scratching and clawing for her life. My objective, in those moments, would be to inflict pain on him, just as pain had been inflicted on me. That's the result of speaking from a place of pain. Unleashing the words I had stored up for him would be like bringing a gun to a knife fight. He wasn't prepared for what I had for him. So instead, I brought nothing. I stayed silent. I allowed myself to be stabbed.

He looked me deep in the eyes. "I can take whatever you have to say to me. Just talk to me. Please, don't just go cold on me."

"Then I need you to help me," I told him. "Fight for me to stay in the present. Know that I always want to talk to you. I just need you to help me get started. Don't just ask me if I'm okay. I'll lie. I *will* lie. I need you to confront me. Tell me you know something is wrong. Just help me get the conversation started."

He looked at me with understanding eyes. "I can do that."

Ryan stayed true to his word. In the weeks and months to follow, when my icy side would start to show, Ryan ignored my physical cues and stood by my side.

"Babe, don't go cold on me. I know what's going on here; you're not okay." He stood firmly by my side and pressed harder. "Something I just said upset you. Look at me. Talk to me. I'm not going anywhere."

It takes more than love to speak my truth

I fully recognize that, as an adult, I probably shouldn't need this type of support. Some might say that by engaging me in this way, Ryan was enabling me to not progress and grow stronger in this area. That may be. But the truth of the matter is that I needed my husband to help me in this very specific way while I was working toward a better way of staying present despite my pain. With time, less and less of Ryan's coaxing was needed for me to express my hurt. He showed me that he could handle what it was I had to say; my pain didn't make him run away from me. He accepted my perspective without questioning why "I let these things get to me," even if he didn't fully understand it. He became safer. I knew he was giving me grace in knowing what I was going through. This new understanding, while not the endgame, would be a game changer.

Chapter 12

One Step Forward, Two Giant Steps Back

Things were definitely on an upswing for Ryan and me. We had taken a huge step forward in a positive direction. I started feeling more emotionally safe with him; I felt safe allowing him to see my pain in whatever form it came out, knowing that he had a better idea of where I was coming from. I felt confident in his ability to guard it safely. While October, November, and December were normally months when the stress of seeing Ryan's family for the holidays would slowly build up, this year was different. I felt seen by him in a new way, and we shared a connectedness deeper than anything previously experienced. This joy and comfort in my marriage consumed my thoughts and was enough to keep most of the stress at bay.

I decided to give therapy another try. I wanted to find someone who could definitively tell me if I was in fact struggling with racial trauma and who could help me cope. I was eager to get started, but the calendar year was coming to an end, and my deductible would soon reset. If anyone is in crisis, I do not advise putting therapy on hold for the purpose of maximizing insurance benefits; but since I was not in crisis and I was two weeks away from the new year, I decided I could wait fourteen days to start my diligent search for a new therapist.

The week leading up to Christmas was when the stress of seeing Ryan's family finally broke through my dam of joy. I started running around and digging into whatever task I could find. It was my way of masking the anxiety I had. This would be the first time that Ryan's entire immediate family came together since Jewel's marriage to Lucy three years prior. We were all anticipating awkwardness and hoping for zero conflicts. While I welcomed Jewel's return to family events, I was kicking myself for not taking a firmer stance against having this reunion happen in my home.

This new understanding of racial trauma and how Ryan's family played a role in it was major, but not major enough to cancel plans that had already been put in motion. I suppose I had renewed hope in Ryan's ability to respond to his family now that he could articulate the type of pain I felt when with them. If he understood trauma, he'd see how imperative it would be to put an end to harmful conversations, right? But with the way I was feeling in those days leading up to their arrival, no amount of reassurance could have made me feel better about them coming. Lucy made the right call and decided to sit this Christmas out. In a desperate, last-minute attempt at emotional self-preservation, I searched for airline tickets so I could leave the city and spend this time with her. But the plane tickets were exorbitantly expensive. So, I was stuck with only my self-talk to comfort me.

I just have to make it through forty-eight hours. I can do that, right? I'll take breaks as needed. It's OK to run errands. I won't let them steal my joy. I'll stay present for my kids. This is my house. This is my safe place.

As we went from hours to mere minutes of their anticipated arrival time, I found myself sitting in my oversized armchair, wrapped up in a blanket, and reading a book: my happy place. The kids were glued to the front windows gasping at each car that came down our street and sighing in disappointment when it wasn't Grandma and Grandpa. Finally, the gasps turned to shrieks of joy which made my heart race and the pit of my stomach hurt. I closed my book, no longer able to concentrate on a single word. They were here.

I willed myself out of my seat to greet them as they got to the room. Fake smiles. Loose embraces.

"Hey, Jenn," Ryan's dad said. "Good to see you."

"You too. How was the drive?"

"Good."

Then came awkward silence as we realized we'd exhausted the conversation and it had only been two minutes. Thank goodness for kids who are willing and ready to fill any silent space with their noises and antics. With the kids serving as a welcome distraction, I was able to sit back down and disappear into my book. Back in my safe, happy place. *I can do this.*

The problem with my safe, happy place was that it was designed for one, with the intention of protecting only one. Like the errands that I claimed I needed to run, I was the sole benefactor of these reprieves. My acts of protecting myself took me away from my kids and any chance I had at protecting them. I was absent. I wasn't there.

I wasn't there at the kitchen table when my daughter sat down and asked to play with Jewel's hair while her grandpa looked on.

"*Tía*, can I do your hair?"

"Sure, honey!"

Grandpa laughed. "Yeah, why don't you give her some cornrows!"

Jewel shot him a look. "Dad!"

My daughter, with a head full of curls, usually wears her hair styled in French braids, buns, or curly puffs. She didn't know what cornrows were, nor did she understand the overtones of the exchange. She looked on in confusion.

I wasn't there in that moment. I wasn't there for that subtle remark that thankfully went over my daughter's head. This was the tough part of prioritizing my self-preservation—it was moments like those that made me realize how vulnerable it left my children. It pained me to think about how many other unhealthy or hurtful remarks I may have missed. It left my heart aching. How many negative comments were made in Ryan's presence that he didn't know to shut down? How many harmful statements still swim around in the consciousness of my kids?

On that visit, thankfully, time was faithful and didn't slow down. The minutes ticked on, and we reached the final night of our Christmas weekend. The kids had been put to bed, and the adults decided to play a card game. We sat around our kitchen table; Ryan was seated to my right, and Jewel was to my left at the head of the table. My brother-in-law sat directly across from me, and his dad next to him. Ryan's mom sat at the other end of the table across from her daughter. The game was a welcome distraction. Everyone would be focused, leaving little room for conversation. There were only the occasional competitive remarks or jokes that elicited a few chuckles. The game lasted nine rounds, and with each passing round, we inched closer to the end of the night. *I can do this. Almost done.*

As the last few cards were laid down and the points totaled up, I didn't concern myself with who won. The night was winding down, and in just a few hours, the weight of having Ryan's parents in my home would be lifted. As Ryan's dad gathered up all of the cards to put away in the box, I could feel myself start to relax. *It's just a matter of time before they push their chairs back from the table and go down to the guest room for the night.*

Except the sound of chair legs sliding across the floor didn't come. Instead, my father-in-law began to lead his family in Christian hymns.

For many years, Ryan's family had enjoyed singing church songs together. Between the five of them, all the major harmonic parts are present, and they can all sing pretty well. They were singing songs and making harmonies that I didn't know. These weren't the songs I grew up singing in my church. And even the ones I recognized sounded unfamiliar. Ryan's family sang the songs as they were written, the notes emblazoned in their minds. Growing up in a Black church with gospel music at its core, I was used to songbirds who sang the notes that the Spirit elicited in the moment. In my church, notes on a page were just a suggestion. The sense of togetherness being cultivated in that moment among the members of Ryan's family didn't include me. Feeling like an outsider in my own home, I sat and tried to put on my best smile to feign enjoyment. The only thing I could think to do was slyly take out my phone and start texting Lucy to tell her what was going on. She would get it. She would understand.

Outsider status at an all-time high.

Feeling like an outsider was commonplace, but it was getting old. I felt like a fool being the only one not singing but knew it would be a jerky move to get up and leave the room.

Eventually, the hymns died down and the table fell quiet. It was a silence just begging to be broken. A topic that was easily accessible to everyone at the table was current events and politics. Ryan's mom grabbed her tablet to play *Township*, a game in which the player farms and builds cities. She kept one foot in reality by looking up from time to time at those of us seated around the table, adding her two cents when she felt like it. I mostly kept my head down and continued texting Lucy.

Conversation is getting tense-ish.

I don't know how it happened, but the conversation turned to Jewel attempting to teach her parents about the generational effects of slavery on the Black community. It was an idea they completely dismissed. Here I was, the only Black person seated at a table full of white people, and they were debating whether or not the consequences of slavery are still felt today. With my eyes locked on my phone in my lap, I marveled at how I ever ended up in a situation like this. I felt small, irrelevant, and invisible. Jumbled thoughts were racing through my mind—panic, curiosity wondering what I was going to hear next, rebuttals to what I was hearing. My head started hurting and I could feel myself freezing up. *Does Ryan see me freezing up?*

> Wish you were here.

Instead of taking a posture of listening and being open to a perspective other than their own, Ryan's parents went the predictable route of saying that slavery doesn't matter since it was so long ago.

Jewel pushed back.

"It matters because the attitudes that were present during slavery contribute to the racist ideologies that are present in government!"

I sat there as my "family" debated whether or not racism was systemic. Jewel was emphatic in her speech and offered tangible examples of how racism has affected the Black community and other people of color. Her parents treated it like an intellectual debate, aiming to shoot down her arguments. My husband was silent. I wondered if anyone thought about how being caught in the crossfire of this conversation was affecting me.

Ryan, where are you? Are you going to say anything?

The lawyer in my sister-in-law would not relent. She was fired up, leaning over the table toward her parents.

"What about the Jim Crow laws? Where do you think those came from? White people were legally able to hunt down and kill Black people with no repercussions."

Ryan's dad was unmoved. "What *about* Jim Crow? Jim Crow is over."

"The legacy of Jim Crow is not gone!"

Where are you, Ryan? Do you see me?

I kept my head, focused on my phone. I could feel my insides bubbling.

> Help me.

I kept texting without receiving any response. It was my way of semi-escaping this hell unfolding before me. Sure, Jewel was there, but she was so wrapped up in this verbal battle with her parents—a battle that I suspect she felt was her way of showing up for me, not realizing that my witnessing this ugliness was doing more harm than good. Lucy was the only person who remotely understood the position I was in. She, too, had married into this family of people who didn't want to take the time to get to understand her individual experiences. In fact, not recognizing Jewel's marriage to another woman as a legitimate union, Ryan's mom barely acknowledged Lucy's existence. Lucy was a safe person who knew what it felt like to be bonded by marriage to this group of people who felt nothing like family.

Frustrated, Jewel turned the conversation to contemporary politics. "You claim to be Christians, but you support a man who locks kids in cages. What about loving your neighbor? *Those* are our neighbors!"

Ryan's mom looked up from her tablet. "Those are *not* my neighbors! My neighbors are in Fargo, North Dakota!" She looked back down at her game, continuing to erect small, virtual communities while the one right in front of her fell apart.

Unbelievable. I glanced at Ryan out of the corner of my eye. *Why aren't you saying anything?*

I felt paralyzed, unable to say anything. It was distressing enough to hear them shoot their daughter down. There was no way I was going to make myself a target for their apathy. Each time they dismissed the very real pain felt by Black and brown communities, it felt like they were dismissing my own personal pain associated with race. Each time they failed to empathize with a community that wasn't their own, I felt less and less confident in their ability to grow into a safe space for me and my kids.

A buzz in my hand—oh glorious buzz! My messages have been seen.

> Omg I can't believe I missed your texts!!!! I'm so sorry!!!

A small sense of relief washed over me. I felt a little less alone even though Lucy was hundreds of miles away. Someone was there—someone who cared about what I was experiencing and how I was experiencing it.

After that, there are whole parts of the conversation that I can't recall. I only remember that Jewel started cussing at her parents, and her parents threw those same, heavy words right back at her. My heart started racing, and I winced at each exchange. I had long known that some parents and kids interacted like this, but I had never witnessed these fights, emotions and all. I was just thankful that my kids were safely tucked away upstairs, sleeping, missing all of this.

I remember thinking how brave my sister-in-law was in spite of the discomfort I felt at hearing how they spoke to one another. She was doing it. She was laying before them some of the grievances I had always wanted to express. The floodgates were open. And I remember when the conversation shifted to become deeply personal for her. I could feel it. She was going to go there. She was going to address the herd of elephants in the room. She was going to call her parents out on disappearing from her life when she told them she was getting married to a woman.

"You abandoned me. You chose to opt out of my life." She looked dead at her mother. "You called me disgusting."

My heart raced and I held my breath as I looked up, my eyes moving from woman to woman. Jewel's lip was quivering. Her mom was still looking down at her tablet. My insides were dying as I sat there listening to a child plead for her parents to understand the damage they had done.

Jewel didn't stop. "You chose to bring me into this world."

Her mother glanced up from her tablet. "Not really. You were accident number two." She gave a small chuckle and looked back down at her game.

I cannot believe this is my family.

Then, finally, the silent man at my side decided to speak. "Not the time for jokes, Mom."

I was dumbfounded. *Is that really all you have to say?*

Jewel continued. "I almost took my life because of the horrible things you said to me."

Finally, Ryan's mom put her tablet down. "Let me go get my hearing aids. I'm only hearing half of what you're saying."

Are you serious right now? We've been having this tense conversation all this time, and you won't even give us the dignity to try to hear more than fifty percent of what is being said?

We took a short intermission of sorts as I continued texting Lucy. I didn't know what else to do. Without documenting this, I'd never believe it actually happened.

Blood boiling, I was hoping that a break in the conversation would serve as an intermission to this monstrosity of a show. People could take a walk, use the bathroom, stretch out their legs and return calmly for the second act. If we were lucky, someone would come back to the table distracted, and we would move on to something else completely, forgetting that we were even engaged in such a discussion. But that didn't happen. Instead, this was a boxing match, with both fighters going to their corners. Instead of calming down, they got more and more amped up as they waited for the next round to begin.

Round two started with Jewel confronting her parents with their lack of hospitality. They insisted that they were great at welcoming people. With her hearing aids in, Ryan's mom was at the ready and jumped into the conversation whenever she could.

"Look at my work with the community garden. I welcome immigrants to come and plant their seeds and teach them about food that can be cultivated in North Dakota. We are very welcoming people."

You are very welcoming people? You? Welcoming?

In a flash, I was taken back to the very first time I visited Ryan's home in Fargo. It was right after the New Year, and I woke up that first morning to a city under a blanket of snow. We had just finished eating the customary bacon and pancakes that Ryan's dad makes every Saturday morning, and Ryan and his younger brother were putting on their winter gear to go out and shovel.

With Ryan's parents in their bedroom getting dressed for the day, I took advantage of this first moment alone in my new settings to assess the situation. *I think it's going well enough so far. They're a little stiffer than I'm used to, but they seem nice enough.* The house felt cold, literally and figuratively. I couldn't help but compare it to what I would have been experiencing if I were back home. Whereas I was positive my mom had music playing and a candle burning, the stillness and quiet here was unsettling. The smell of bacon lingered and the only sound that broke the silence was the movement of the second hand of the clock that hung on the wall.

"Where's Ryan?" I was jilted from my thoughts by Ryan's mom, her tight curls still shedding sporadic water droplets as she came into the kitchen and started preparing her morning cup of Café Vienna.

"Oh, they went outside to shovel the driveway."

She stopped stirring her coffee and looked at me. "And what about you? Are your arms broken?"

Welcoming? Yeah, right.

Back in the present, at the kitchen table that night, Jewel wasn't backing down. "My wife doesn't feel like part of the family."

Ryan's dad spoke up. "She's a beautiful young lady, and I love her."

"Well, I can tell you that it doesn't feel welcoming for her. The little acknowledgement that you give her feels like scraps compared to the warmth she is used to."

Silence. The perfect entry point for Ryan. I willed him to enter into the fray. *Don't leave your sister hanging. Back her up on this. You know they haven't been welcoming to me either.* Silence. Silence. More silence. Of all the times when he had been silent, all the times when he had claimed he couldn't do anything because the moment had passed, none of those times felt as egregious as this one. Ryan and I were just coming off of crossing some huge bridges toward a better understanding of one another. With the new understanding that Ryan was showing me, I had started to put trust in his promise to shield me from and speak up against his family's ignorance. He was different now. *We* were different now. But this conversation showed me that when the situation arose, when his moment to shine appeared, Ryan was nowhere to be seen or heard.

And then I heard it—I heard him take a breath, and at last he began to speak.

"Well, how can we move forward? Where can we come together? I mean, Mom, I think it's fair to assume that you won't ever acknowledge that your daughter has a wife, right?"

She shook her head firmly. "No, I will not. It violates my principles."

"OK, that's fair. So what *can* we agree on?"

I was on the verge of tears and wishing so badly I weren't there. I felt let down. Each time Ryan stayed silent, he was proving to me that he was not able to stand up to his parents. Only two months earlier, we'd had this breakthrough about trauma—specifically my trauma as it pertains to racism. And here his parents were arguing about slavery and Jim Crow. Here they were rejecting other humans as their neighbors simply because they resided on the other side of a national border. I expected that Ryan would hear these things and recognize them as triggers for me. I had allowed myself to believe he was going to show up in the way that I, with all of my heart, needed him to. I was waiting for something that wasn't going to happen.

I tried to keep Lucy updated on the goings-on of the conversation, but at that point, my heart was so deflated and had sunk so low with disappointment that my messages tapered off. My own thoughts consumed me, fading out the conversation going on around me. I sat there stunned, not only by the nature of the conversation, but by Ryan's silence. The door had been opened for him to stand up to his parents. He even had an ally in his sister so that he wouldn't have to bear the brunt of the fight alone. He was presented with opportunity after opportunity to interject and show me that he believed differently than his parents, and he let them pass him by like speedway racers at the Indy 500. He was a spectator glued to his seat. He was proud of his sister for speaking up, but not willing to enter the conversation in any role other than that of the mediator. More concerned about his parents' feelings than those of the woman with whom he shared his bed night after night, he chose silence. Silence. Silence that made the five inches between us feel more like five hundred miles. I thought we had made this great leap in our marriage, but it felt like we were moving backward.

My thoughts were disturbed when laughter erupted at the table. I was lost, having tuned out of the final moments of the conversation. I just assumed that Ryan had excelled at his role of mediating the tension right out of the room. *Bravo, Ryan. You made them all feel comfortable again.*

Chairs started to push back from the table as it was announced it was time for bed. It had been a big moment for my sister-in-law, and she seemed satisfied. Her victory came in speaking the words she had bottled up inside of her. And for the entire family, who avoided big emotions and sidestepped tough issues, living through that tense conversation made them feel like they had actually achieved some great feat—like they'd had a breakthrough moment as a family.

"And let's get the hugs going!" Jewel jovially shouted as she stretched her arms out wide.

I was flabbergasted. There are moments of conflict that serve as an impetus for change and healing, but that was not what I had just witnessed. They yelled at each other, had nasty exchanges, and Ryan doused the fire to bring them all back down to Earth. As far as I could see, they would leave this conversation the same people they were when they entered it.

Celebrating what he thought was a growth moment for everyone in the room, Ryan's dad pulled me into a tight embrace while saying, "Thank you." I raised my limp arms just enough to put my fingertips on his back. I pulled away when it felt appropriate only to be passed to Ryan's mom who gave me a big kiss on my cheek. Maybe they all felt closer as a result of what had just happened, but I felt like I was falling further and further away from any hope of connecting with this family, Ryan's parents in particular.

The next morning, I had just enough energy to help my kids get breakfast before parking myself in my favorite chair with my nose in a book. The kids noticed I was a bit standoffish, but I explained to them that I was tired from being up late the night before. They accepted that answer and left me to myself in my safe space. Agitated, but content to be left alone, the sound of my father-in-law's voice interrupted the pseudo calm I was experiencing.

"Jenn, it was good to see you."

I lifted my gaze to see Ryan's parents standing in front of me, coats on, ready to go.

"Have a safe drive."

They thought I was being disrespectful by not walking them to the door with a courteous sendoff, but I was so distraught about what I had witnessed the night before that I couldn't fake it. Usually, I was able to maintain some level of interaction with everyone while in the presence of Ryan's family, but the silence and withdrawal that typically follows our time together came early. Even my sister-in-law, who remained after Ryan's parents and brother left, was confused by my silence.

She interpreted the walls I had put up around myself as my being upset with her, but I wasn't. She had never seen me in the aftermath of spending time with my in-laws. Ryan, on the other hand, recognized this behavior very well. This time he knew it was because I was triggered. Days later he would tell me, "I knew I was supposed to say something that night at the table. I knew my silence was bothering you."

I told myself that I had to remain hopeful that he would one day grow into a person who could stand up for me to his family in the moment when I needed him. Though the level of hopefulness ebbed and flowed, I maintained hope because the thought of ceasing to have any was too painful to bear. I could tell that Ryan wanted to protect me in the way that I needed. He had graduated to being able to recognize when something was bothering me. But he didn't know how to speak up against these things, and I still found myself drowning in the wake of his silence and my own.

When I confronted him about what he could have said to support his sister and stand up to the ugly things I had encountered in his family, it was like a light bulb came on. At the same time, disappointment washed over his face because he didn't think of it himself.

That evening with his family taught me that someone can understand a problem and still not know what to do with it, no matter how badly they wanted to. I had hoped that the words of their son, whom they loved and respected, could reach them in a way that mine never would. But he just wasn't there yet, and I was beginning to panic and wonder if he ever would be. I was desperate for him to get there.

It takes more than love to keep history from repeating itself

Nearly a decade. That's how much time had passed since the first time I was shocked into a silence that gave way to rage when I spent my first Christmas with Ryan and his family. Nearly a decade. That's how long I had been struggling to cope with the pain consistently brought on by my time with them. Nearly a decade. That's how long I went back and forth between wondering if this was something I was taking too personally and knowing that their actions and words were unacceptable and needed to be addressed.

I had witnessed a shockingly painful conversation where I heard a lack of compassion toward other people. It was a conversation that would make me question what I was doing sharing my life and my children with people who couldn't (wouldn't?) see past physical differences to recognize the humanity in all of us. A conversation that, as in other moments, my husband tolerated.

A decade ago, I had been knocked down, but I popped back up with the desperate optimism of a newlywed not ready to give up. I'd had countless conversations with Ryan in hopes of furthering his understanding of the harm that unaddressed ignorance can have on people—and on me. I'd hoped our conversations would change how interactions with his family went, but it seemed that our talks had hardly moved the needle.

This time, his family depleted me of every last ounce of strength and hope I had as I once again willed myself to be OK around Ryan's family even if none of them ever made an effort to understand my position among them. This time, I had to ask myself how I could keep the next ten years from being like the last.

Chapter 13

Things Weren't Fine–Therapy, Take Two

I did hope that things would eventually smooth themselves out as they usually did once his parents were gone long enough, but things weren't fine. And they didn't become fine. My feeling of numbness turned to anger and bitterness. This time was different. I now had a better understanding of what was happening to me emotionally when I was with Ryan's family. And I knew that Ryan knew it too. His inaction and silence crushed me; it chipped away at the trust I had in him to act in our family's best interest. Losing that trust meant losing my sense of emotional safety in his presence.

A therapist! He was a therapist, for goodness' sake, and he didn't step in to interrupt that toxic conversation. Needless to say, The Ice Queen overtook me with full force and reduced me to one-word interactions with him in the immediate aftermath of Christmas. Whenever we attempted to talk about what had happened, I was too angry and hurt to see anything from his perspective. Ryan recognized the gravity of the situation.

By day, he tried to keep things light and normal for the sake of our kids while I avoided his every touch and gaze—also for the sake of the kids. I couldn't risk blowing up at him in front of them. Thank God for the self-absorbed nature of young kids who run around concerned with only themselves and their own interests. It served as a small comfort to know that they weren't catching on to the distance between their parents.

By night, Ryan drew closer to me, trying to penetrate The Ice Queen's wall of silence.

"Jenn, we will get through this."

"To be clear, I'm only here because I keep my promises, and we have kids." *And if we didn't have the kids, I'm not sure I would honor this vow.* I couldn't bring myself to allow that thought to slip past my lips. Though it was a very real truth, I was afraid that if I voiced it, we wouldn't be able to recover from it. So, in my head it remained. I was still committed to making my marriage work and to exhausting *all* possible options toward that end.

It was useless to move forward without the help of a professional—one that I was not married to. January 1st thankfully came around, and I started the search for a therapist. This time around, it was a completely different experience. I took the lessons I had learned from my previous stint in therapy to fine-tune my search.

Although I was using the same site I had used to find my last therapist, the experience was completely different. This time around, I checked boxes I would never have thought applied to me—trauma, PTSD, EMDR. There also seemed to be new categories. I indicated that I was struggling with racial identity. I even checked the box next to "multicultural" without really knowing what that meant. If there was a chance that I could find a therapist of color, I wanted to check all the boxes that would ensure that outcome.

I clicked the search button and held my breath.

I breathed a sigh of relief when Ryan's face was not the first image offered to me this time. Even more exciting was that my results page was flooded with men and women of color, each face representing opportunities of hope and healing. This time I didn't scroll through pictures and rely solely on vibes. I looked through their profiles, read bios and specialties, and settled on one who seemed like a good fit. I composed an email.

> Hi, I'm looking for help with an ongoing issue in my 10-year marriage. I am a Black woman married to a white man whose family is prejudiced and ignorant. I experienced deep hurts at the hands of his family members early on in our marriage that I haven't recovered from, and each time I see them the hurt is just compounded. My husband is ill-equipped to handle it, and I'm barely functioning as a result of incidents from this past Christmas with them. It gets worse and worse as time goes on. Do you think you might be able to walk with me through this? I need help.

I clicked send, hoping that it would be the beginning of a journey to healing. Five hours later, I got a response.

> Thank you for your email. I have worked with several interracial couples with these very issues. I think it is important to address these issues within the marriage and extended family. I would like to work with you as you process through the hurt.

Thank you, Jesus.

Two weeks later, I walked into Sophia's office for my first session. Nerves and desperation had gotten the best of me, and I entered with tears already forming even before I officially told my story. I walked in, sat down on her couch, and started from the very beginning.

"We met about twelve and a half years ago . . ."

The tears began to fall as I relived the previous decade of interactions with Ryan's family. Sophia's gentle eyes and soft expression let me know that she could hear and feel the pain I had inside of me. She not only met my vulnerability with care, but it was also clear that she understood the things I was saying as well as the deeper messages that lay beneath the surface. Sometimes her eyes opened really wide in shock and disbelief when I repeated words or phrases spoken in my presence. This was so different from when I said those things to Ryan and he hadn't reacted at all. I could tell that she got it, and it felt so good to be got.

"You're definitely dealing with a lot of pain, and I do believe you're being impacted by racial trauma."

I slowly nodded my head, letting her words sink in. "I'm nervous that there isn't healing for me."

"Oh, no. There is healing for you. I think it would be good to do EMDR with you, but we can't start with that."

"OK," I said hesitantly.

"First, we need to get you and your husband to a better place. You need new patterns of communication. We need to repair that relationship first."

My eyes narrowed in confusion.

She continued, "As we dig into your racial trauma, it is going to leave you raw. It's going to be emotionally grueling. You will walk through your racial trauma so that we can re-process those experiences in a healthier way. You will go home exhausted. You will go home emotionally depleted. I need you to go home to a healthy relationship. So, we're going to work on your marriage first. It would be unethical of me to do otherwise."

"OK," I said, nodding and sounding more upbeat. "I get that." Not only did I get that, but I was also awestruck by the wisdom that Sophia showed. It totally made sense.

"Your homework for tonight is to go home and tell Ryan that he needs to get himself a therapist."

My eyes got big. "Really?" *Ha! He's messed up too!*

"Oh Honey, yes. Ryan needs to get himself a therapist. You're not completely innocent in all of this, but if he'd had the tools to speak up to his parents, you wouldn't have had to go through some of the things you went through. He needs to explore this. Plus, he's going to need someone to talk to as he learns to be a support to you while you go through this process."

"OK, that won't be a problem. Ryan's like the one person in the world who will be excited to go to therapy. He's always wanted to try it."

"Truth be told, Ryan should have been in therapy a long time ago. All therapists need a therapist."

"So will you be his therapist?"

"Noooooo," she said emphatically. "I don't see therapists."

I laughed. For the first time in weeks, I laughed. And for the first time in weeks, I felt hope.

That night, Ryan and I sat down to debrief about my time with Sophia. He was eager to hear how it went, and I was just as excited to talk to him about it.

"She said you need to go to therapy."

"Oh. Umm, okay. Did she say why?"

I recounted the conversation Sophia and I had about what Ryan would get out of seeing a therapist of his own.

"Okay. Yeah," he said. "That makes sense."

"Look, Ryan. If we're going to have a fighting chance at moving past this together, we have to rewrite the way we operate as a couple."

He nodded enthusiastically. "Okay."

"I don't think you understand what this has done to me. I have no trust in you right now, and I don't feel close to you. If this is going to work, we need to start all the way over. We need to get to know each other in a new way as we do our work in therapy. I need to fall in love with you again. I don't want to mend what's broken. I want to build something new."

Yes, we had been married for ten years. Yes, we had four children. Yes, we had a household to run together. It wasn't going to be easy, but I was convinced that we needed to dismantle as much of our marriage as we could and completely rebuild our relationship.

"So, what do you think?" I asked. "Is that something you can do? Will you go to therapy?"

"Yes. Of course. I'm all in. Whatever it takes."

It takes more than love to start the journey of healing

Ryan and I had to recognize that our foundation had cracks too deep to withstand what we were up against and what lay ahead for us. I approached therapy as a singular journey, but I quickly realized that it was undeniably a journey that the two of us would go on together. For real, long-lasting change, it could never be a solo journey. A deep change like the one I was seeking had to include the one with whom I was most intimate. My first session with Sophia made me realize that this would change everything for me, for Ryan, and for my kids. Little did I know, the ripple effects of change would reach far beyond my little family and me.

Chapter 14

Let's Get to Work

2020 was going to be the year we worked toward real healing, not just quick, temporary fixes. It wasn't going to be fun, but it was necessary and I believed it would ultimately revolutionize our marriage.

Sophia maintained that she wouldn't do couples counseling, nor would she take Ryan on as a client. But when Ryan reached out to her in a moment of frustration, feeling desperate to understand me, she agreed to sit down with him. During my session that immediately followed the time they spent together, Sophia spelled out a major reason why I still felt unheard and misunderstood even after having lengthy conversations with Ryan: he actually wasn't hearing and understanding what I was saying. Plain and simple. And it was likely I wasn't understanding everything he was expressing either.

"My communication is driven by emotion, while yours is driven by logic and reason," I said to Ryan.

He chewed on that for a moment. "OK, I can see that. Say more."

"I don't only rely on words to communicate. If someone is talking to me, sure, their words are telling me things. But the way they are saying it and their expressions give me a lot of information too. But it's not that way for you, is it?"

"No, not really. I want to know the facts. The emotion gets in the way."

"It's like white noise for you."

He nodded. "Exactly. Emotions don't give me all the information I need to know. Like I said, I need the facts. I need the details. I need the words."

I sighed, then continued.

"For our everyday conversations, we communicate just fine. But when my emotions are running high, I sometimes don't have adequate words. And that's when I'm counting on you to decipher my facial expressions or my body language to understand what I'm trying to get through to you."

Ryan shook his head and shrugged. "Growing up, I was never taught that emotions were an asset, something to pay attention to. When I was upset, I would get sent to my room and told not to come out until I was happy again."

My heart sank for that little boy. "Your parents are the worst."

He chuckled. "They just don't know what to do with emotions, and I guess I still have some learning to do on that as well."

"Says the therapist!" I smiled, nudging him half in jest and half in genuine bewilderment. "I know you're a great therapist for those who just need the facts, but I'd hate to have you as a therapist."

He smiled. "You're probably right."

"Well, Sophia said we need to start working toward meeting each other in the middle. I'll start putting more words to my emotions, and you can start tapping into your emotional side a bit more."

An opportunity for me to lean into my logic came pretty quickly. Normally, Valentine's Day was not a big deal for Ryan and me. We thought the spirit of the holiday should be present in every day of our marriage. But given that we were trying to rebuild our relationship and the day happened to fall on a Friday, we decided to take the opportunity to make it a special night. I got excited when Ryan said he would plan something, because I'm normally the one to take the lead in making plans.

Well, Friday night came, and no plans had been made. It was a normal at-home evening. We ate a run-of-the-mill dinner with our four very loud kids making absurd noises around a table spattered with condiments and fruit juices. Then I endured an unromantic, exhausting evening where kids argued and hung on me; my only reprieve came at bedtime after a struggle to shut down additional requests for water, trips to the bathroom, and that sixth or seventh "I can't sleep without it" hug. It wasn't at all what I had hoped. It felt silly to even care, but I did. Ryan didn't do what he'd said he'd do. Hurt and disappointment flooded my heart, and I could feel The Ice Queen slowly creeping in.

After seeing the huge difference in our communication styles, Sophia had given me Emotion Regulation worksheets. She advised me to take them out whenever I felt myself emotionally retreating from Ryan. Now that I knew he couldn't recognize and utilize my emotions, I needed to put words to what I was feeling. My heart growing evermore icy toward him, I grabbed my stack of sheets.

"Ryan, can you come sit with me?"

"Sure, babe."

A nervous silence ensued as I flipped through the sheets looking for the one that described the emotion I was feeling; Ryan sat patiently, not sure what I was doing. *Here it is. Sadness.* I took a deep breath and stumbled through the prompts and verbiage options, never once looking up for a reaction.

"I feel disappointed. I feel this way because I was told you would plan a special evening for us, and that didn't happen. So, this night did not turn out the way I expected."

I paused. *This isn't me. It feels robotic. I feel so weird doing this.* I continued. "When something like this happens, it makes me feel like

I won't be able to get what I need or want from you. This emotion makes me low in energy, and I feel a hollowness in my chest. My sadness presents as moping, withdrawing, talking very little, and using a quiet voice. As a result, I will ruminate about other similar things you've done in the past that disappointed me."

I relaxed the muscles that I didn't even realize I was clenching. I stared at the paper for a few seconds before slowly and nervously turning to look at Ryan. My eyes were met with a soft expression of deep concern.

"Jenn, I didn't realize you were so hurt."

I was shocked. "You understood that?"

"Of course I did."

Oh my gosh. These sheets are magic. Ryan apologized for letting me down. The next night, he arranged for my parents to watch the kids, and he took me to a really nice dinner, sans fruit juices and farting noises.

It wasn't long before I was able to communicate with Ryan without the prompts and word choices from the sheets. The main point was to walk him through what I was experiencing when I had an emotion. When I started to feel something, I told him what prompted the feeling, explained my interpretation of the prompting event, and described what happened to me physically when I felt the emotion. I explained how the emotion within me presented to everyone else and the aftereffects of feeling that way. It felt like I was overcomplicating something as simple as an emotion. But for Ryan, it was a lifeline. It was what he needed, and it changed the way we communicated.

As for Ryan, he couldn't start expressing his emotions overnight. He first started by really looking at my emotions and recognizing them as a form of communication. On my journey to permanently thawing The Ice Queen, she still managed to make a cameo every once in a while. On one such occasion, I slipped back into my normal jam of self-protecting through emotional withdrawal. This time my husband was ready to interrupt.

"Jenn, what's going on?"

"Nothing. I'm fine."

Ryan planted his feet firmly and stared into my eyes. "I hear you telling me you're fine, but your face is showing me something else. Please don't go away from me."

Any hardened exterior I was attempting to show completely broke down as I tearfully fell into his arms. Tearful because he was paying attention. Tearful because he saw that the authentic me was hurting. Tearful because he pursued me. Tearful because he stayed. Tearful because we were making progress.

Equipped with a new way of connecting and communicating, Sophia tasked us with implementing a weekly check-in. The idea was to make it impossible for either of us to stew and withhold hurt feelings from the other for too long. It consisted of three questions:

1. What is something I did this week that you would love to see more of?

2. What is something I did this week that you wouldn't mind seeing less of?

3. Is there anything pending that we need to talk about?

We played around with the format and the wording, but ultimately stuck with the three questions above.

I never would have considered us a couple who didn't spend quality time together. With four kids and our daily grind akin to two ships passing in the night, we were very aware of the need to make the most of the time we had together. We had always been very intentional about that. Even so, it was astounding how quickly we saw the benefits of an intentional check-in. It gave us an opportunity to give one another compliments when we may have taken a nice gesture or kind words for granted in the past.

"I've really liked getting texts from you each day during lunchtime just to see how I'm doing. I would love to see more of that."

It also gave us space to air even the smallest grievances that we would have otherwise just sat on.

"I could use less of finding your little beard hairs around the sink after you've trimmed. It grosses me out."

Sometimes the pending things were big; other times they were small things that we kept putting on the back burner. This intentional, scripted entry point into dialogue often led to much deeper conversations beyond those three prompts. We almost always ended the evening feeling more connected and loving toward one another. Setting aside this time to connect was powerful. It was always after the kids went to bed, and we never planned anything else for that night. We had all the time in the world for each other.

It was during those conversations that some of our biggest breakthroughs were achieved. New levels of understanding were reached. Walls were dismantled. It was in those times that I saw my husband, the man who rarely cried, become acquainted with tears. And cry he did. Sometimes to the point where he couldn't make it stop.

"Ryan, I just feel like you censor yourself around me."

He sighed. "It's not just you. I do it with everyone."

"I'm not 'everyone.' I'm your wife."

"Yeah, I know."

"But why do you do it?" I asked him.

"I don't know. I just hold things back things that I don't think people will find interesting."

"Ryan, it's me. Your wife. Even if it's not interesting to me, I'm still interested because of who you are to me."

He gave an unbelieving, half smile. "Thanks, babe."

"I'm serious! This is what unconditional love is. I want to know every part of you. I'm always interested. That's what it means to be family."

His tears started to fall. "I've never had that." I pulled him into a comforting embrace, my heart breaking for him while at the same time harboring frustration toward his parents. I was starting to make connections and understand how the emotionally distant parenting Ryan received turned him into the man I held in my arms in that moment.

During another check-in, Ryan was able to put words to one of his defense mechanisms in a way that surprised even him.

"My way of protecting myself is to let things slide off my back. I don't allow myself to get offended, so it's hard to take anything personally. But when I have someone like you, who expects to be protected, my self-protection leaves you completely vulnerable."

We'd committed to creating a new dynamic between us, and it was happening. Our moments of being open and raw with one another during these intentional conversations were the foundational corner-stones in the reconstruction of our marriage as the new people we were becoming. Ryan's dedication to accessing and embracing emotion as productive was affirming for me. My resolve to make the effort to put into words what I was feeling was helpful to him. We didn't always do it right, but we promised we would stick with it.

From early on, we could tell these check-ins would lead us down a promising path. Instead of doing it just once a week, we made it a twice-weekly event. It's something we continue to this day, and it continues to lead us into deeper trust and intimacy within a marriage built on a firmer foundation.

It takes more than love to communicate with the one you love

Ryan and I had to really unpack our preferred ways of communicating. We had to examine not only how it affected the way we expressed ourselves, but also how we received what was being expressed to us. Then we came together and discovered how our communication styles interacted and affected our interactions with each other. All this time, I had thought Ryan was this man with little to no emotion. All it took was meeting him halfway, and pushing him to do the same, for me to realize that he had emotions that he was just never encouraged to access. I reflected on the many times I had felt hurt or angry because I had shared something upsetting with Ryan and his reaction didn't meet my expectations of joining in my pain or ire. Learning more about his understanding of the utility of emotions put things into perspective for me, and I no longer judged how he felt about something based on his seemingly disconnected way of discussing a topic. It allowed me to take his lack of a reaction less personally.

Ryan never wanted me to feel like I was alone in my struggles. As a problem-solver, he thought he was doing the best for me by sticking to the facts and finding a solution. But many times, I just wanted his empathy. I wanted him to feel for me and with me. And when he couldn't do that, I interpreted it as a lack of connection, a lack of love.

Every day I'm grateful to Sophia for giving us the tools to push past what was preventing us from communicating effectively.

Chapter 15

Breakthrough

Ⓦe had no way of knowing that 2020 would also be the year in which the whole world turned upside down. Shortly into March, it became evident that the Covid-19 virus was making its way through the U.S. and every other part of the world. Schools and businesses were shutting their doors, and everyone was advised to stay at home and quarantine. First, we were told it would only be for a couple of weeks. Later, we were given some arbitrary dates of when things would reopen that came and went, but it eventually became clear that this was going to be our reality for an indefinite amount of time. I remember my last in-person session with Sophia. We would continue work together virtually, but I had no idea when I would sit in her office again. I was nervous about the prospect of being quarantined with Ryan. We were in the early stages of our new trajectory as a couple, and our interactions were still riddled with uncertainty and fear of missteps. The expression on my face made it clear that I found the idea of our constant time together daunting. Sophia, on the other hand, looked giddy.

"Neither of you has anywhere to go," she said as she smiled and clapped her hands. "Whether you like it or not, you're going to have the time you need to work on yourselves and on your marriage. So you might as well take advantage of this moment and do the work."

The Covid-19 pandemic changed a lot of things for us and made normally mundane tasks tricky. We were physically isolated from our friends and families. Both Ryan and I had to learn to do our jobs online—him transitioning clients to online therapy and me figuring out how to make educational videos that would hold the attention of kindergartners. We were constantly searching for ways to keep four children ranging from ages three to eight both entertained and academically challenged. Leaving the house meant risking exposure to other (potentially sick) people and usually resulted in a risk assessment to see if it was worth it. Even so, Sophia ended up being right. Despite its challenges, this new way of living during the pandemic afforded Ryan and me the time and distance we needed from people, commitments, and distractions to be able to work on our marriage.

Even though it wasn't always perfect, there was no denying our overall forward momentum as a result of our individual work with our respective therapists. We felt like a team in a way we hadn't before, probably because the stakes had never been so high. We were both determined to do our work in therapy, knowing that our partner's growth depended on our own and that the fate of our marriage depended on us giving it our all. It wasn't perfect, but we were putting in the work, and I was allowing myself to believe that we really would make it through this and come out stronger and better than we had ever been.

And then George.

It started one morning with his name popping up all over my Instagram feed. I saw hashtag after hashtag with George Floyd's name and Black Lives Matter. *What is all this? What happened? Who is George Floyd?* And then I saw it. With the swipe of a finger, I saw what I couldn't unsee. With the swipe of a finger, a still image came across my screen that will forever haunt me and millions of others around the world. With the swipe of a finger, my heart broke, my soul mourned, and my deepest fears for my brothers, my dad, and my son unapologetically resurfaced.

When I found out that there was a video of the entire murder circulating on the internet, I knew myself enough to know that I didn't want to watch it. I couldn't watch it. My heart wouldn't be able to take it. I am not unaware of police brutality and the racism that fuels it. I know about the over-policing that goes on in Black and brown communities. I am all too familiar with the attempts of officers to police the movements of Black and brown bodies. I, myself, had an encounter on the affluent north side of Chicago in which a white officer asked me what I was doing "way over here". Knowing he thought I belonged on the predominantly Black south side of the city, I simply stated that I venture all over Chicago. I matter-of-factly told him I was a graduate student at the University of Illinois at Chicago and rattled off the exact address of my church, located on the north side. With a slight anger behind my eyes, I looked him square in the face to let him know that I knew what he was doing and that his racism was showing. No, I didn't need to watch the video. It was not going to inform me of something I didn't already know was happening.

George Floyd's murder was a dark cloud that hung over my head. A sadness overcame me. It was only for the sake of my kids that I put on a smile in the days that followed. Every morning, I stuffed my fears, my anger, and my angst down so that I could show up and be present for them as their mom. All day long I denied my emotions until they went to bed; then I would promptly curl up in a blanket and cry. I cried for George. I cried for Ahmaud. I cried for Breonna. I cried for Trayvon. I cried for Emmett. I cried for all of the names I couldn't remember. I cried for all the names I would never know. I cried for all of us.

I was successful in masking how I felt in front of my kids, but there were times when Ryan could see the sadness behind my eyes. "Jenn, are you OK?"

"No. I'm not. Have you heard about George?"

A deep sigh. "I did. It's so sad."

"It's more than sad. It's devastating. Did you watch the video?"

Ryan shook his head. "Just snippets. Not the whole thing. Did you?"

"No. My heart can't take it."

Day in and day out, I had to fight hard to go about my normal routine because our school year wasn't over yet. Classes were over, but I had two weeks of meetings and professional development to complete. Virtual meeting after virtual meeting. Day after day, I sat with my camera on (to be a team player) as the only Black person on my staff. Day after day, I listened to my coworkers' jokes and their lighthearted laughter, saw their smiles, and forced myself to smile even though I was dying inside. Day after day, the loudest thing I heard was the silence regarding George Floyd. No one said a word.

And then one day, I couldn't keep up the facade. It was June 3rd, my son's birthday. My only son's birthday. My sweet, precious, little boy's birthday. I woke up that morning with the sun, as I normally do. It took me a moment to register what day it was.

Oh yes! My sweet boy turns seven today! And then, without warning, *I wonder how many more birthdays he will live to see.*

Shock and horror gave way to devastation as my hand flew to my chest in hopes of calming down my rapidly beating heart. Never had I asked myself that question before, yet in that moment, it seemed like the most natural question to pose. Heavy breathing turned to gasps that became sobs as I realized that nothing I could do would ever keep my Black children, specifically my Black son, safe. There are few things worse than a parent feeling helpless to protecting their children.

I couldn't wallow in my sorrows for too long. I had a virtual meeting with my fellow teachers as well as members of our school administration. The responsibility to facilitate a lot of our meetings had fallen on me, but I just couldn't that day. I texted two of my fellow kindergarten teachers—two women who I knew were safe and wouldn't be surprised to hear what I was going through.

> Good morning, ladies. With everything that is going on, I'm really struggling this morning. I can't stop crying, and I'm having a hard time. I will be at the meeting, but I'm going to have my camera and mic off. Will you please step in and lead this meeting?

I sat through another meeting full of laughter and joy and wondered what it must be like to have the world crashing all around you and feel none of the effects. By the afternoon, I pulled myself together, and we had a beautiful celebration of my son's seventh birthday.

At my first session with Sophia following George Floyd's murder, her face was so sad on my computer screen, and she gave a half smile. I responded in kind.

"Sophia, are you up to doing this session? We don't have to do this; I know you're hurting too."

"Yes, I am hurting. But no, I'm OK. I can do this. Thanks, though."

We moved forward with our hour-long session. At one point we sat silently, looking at each other with teary eyes. We didn't need to use words. We were mourning, together.

"All Ryan said to me was that it was sad. He still doesn't get it, and I don't know what I can do to get him to understand how close to home this is. His family's racism, his inability to step up and squash that—that's how murders like this happen!"

"Has he watched the video?"

"Snippets of it, yes."

Sophia shook her head. "No. You need to ask him to watch the whole thing. Not snippets. The entire thing. He needs to watch all eight minutes and forty-six seconds of it."

"OK . . ." I hesitated.

"Just do it. And when he's done, ask him to picture it being your son instead of George." Always the dutiful therapy client, I agreed.

Ryan was a little surprised when I made the request of him, but without hesitation he said he would watch the video. He snuck away to a quiet room in the house to have some privacy, and I went to go play with our little girls in their bedroom. I was sat there, doing puzzles with the girls, when Ryan walked in about twenty minutes later. He slowly approached us; his face was drained of color. Barely able to lift his gaze, he subtly shook his head in disbelief. I stood to meet him, and he pulled me into a forceful embrace.

"I watched it."

I pulled back to meet his eyes, glistening from tears.

"Now imagine that being our son instead of George."

The impact of that statement was too much for him to bear. Grief-stricken, he eased himself down onto our daughter's bed, his head in his hands. I lowered myself to kneel by him. He looked at me intensely.

"Please, don't ever watch that video," he said.

"I won't. I can't."

"This isn't right. This isn't right. Things have to change."

That moment was *the* moment that it all changed for Ryan. That was the moment he realized that racism wasn't just a thing of the past or something that happens somewhere else to other people. That was the moment he realized how close to home racism hits. That was the moment when he realized that racism was his problem too, and that he had a part to play in dismantling it. That was the moment he formed an emotional connection to the injustices that people of color face in this country.

"I need to figure out what I can do. Is that kind of stuff happening here in Omaha, and we just don't know about it? Who is held accountable? Who is policing the police?"

His questions were many. And for the next several months, he pored over articles, books, webcasts, and more to learn all he could about racism. Without having anticipated it, this was the moment I had been waiting for. Seeing him emotionally affected by the things going on around him gave me a sense of relief because he was able to access this empathy for things happening to other people.

With the relief also came anger. Why was this what it took for him to empathize with communities of color? Why, when he had married a Black woman and created Black children? I resented the privilege that let him live so long without being affected by racism; it had been a part of my reality for as long as I could remember. It didn't seem fair. It *wasn't* fair. Ryan's emotional pain over other people's suffering wasn't fun to witness, but I can't say that I had pity for him. What he was learning as he pushed forty, kids of color had to learn while thirty years his junior. And the stakes were much higher for them.

While I didn't have to pity him, I realized it wasn't helpful for me to give him a hard time for being late to the game. This was his moment of realization. This was the moment I had been desperately waiting for him to have. He was experiencing a period of shock, horror, and mourning as it sank in for him that he was going to start viewing everything through different eyes now. He grew up where he grew up, and the people who raised him were the people who raised him. I couldn't change that, nor could he. His moment of realization came when it came. I still have moments when I get stuck in the fact that it took him so long. But the fact of the matter remains: he had the moment I needed him to have.

Not long after that, Ryan sat down by me on the couch and said, "I know you've told me before about all of the things my family has done to you. Would you mind telling me again? One more time?"

"Like, right now? Are you sure? There's a lot."

"Yes, right now. I want to hear it all."

I went through moment after moment where I had felt singled out by his family and left vulnerable by him. Tearfully, reliving it all, I went through every question and comment that went unchecked. I told him how seeing a Confederate flag on his parents' fridge made me feel. He winced, lowered his eyes, and deeply sighed while shaking his head. I did not tell him anything he had not already heard. He had been there to witness most of what I shared for himself.

His reactions, however, painted a very different picture. It was as if he was hearing it for the first time. "Oh my gosh. That happened, and I didn't say anything? I'm sorry."

As I continued to share, he went on, "I can't believe I didn't say anything. I'm so sorry."

That's when I realized that, in a way, he *was* hearing this for the very first time. Really hearing it. Really hearing *me*. He was hearing it with brand-new ears. He was processing what I was saying through a brand-new lens that he could not remove. He was waking up to a new reality, and it was a nightmare. What was truly painful for him was the role he had played in all of it.

It takes more than love to really see what's been happening all along

I can remember the time Ryan told me about a guest speaker who had visited his college in North Dakota to talk about white privilege. He scoffed at the idea. *What privilege?* He and everyone he knew had worked hard for all that they had. Ryan pushed back against this speaker that he felt was trying to make everyone feel guilty for what they had achieved.

The thing about white privilege is that it's really hard to see your privilege, especially if you're in a monocultural community where you don't see how your acceptance and navigation through society is different from others whose identities don't align with yours. That was the case with Ryan.

Being concerned with "just the facts" for so long, he interpreted people's emotional reactions to painful events as their own personal way of processing the event. He didn't see strong reactions as an indicator of how horrible something was. He could say, "Wow, that was really terrible for *you*," but it didn't translate to being something egregious in general.

Some people need to witness the worst of humanity before they believe a true atrocity is occurring. The video of George's murder was indisputable. Ryan wasn't getting a secondhand account in which he was left to decipher whether or not those telling the story were overstating their case. No. He saw it as it played out, and he was horrified. Not only was this real, it meant that the other stories were real too. It meant my fears were real. It meant that the racism my kids would face was real, as were the potentially dangerous consequences of that racism. It meant that he had been, unknowingly, part of the oppression that ignored the cries. It meant that he was not, up to that point, part of the solution.

Chapter 16

Silence Hurts Every Time

In the wake of George Floyd's murder, protests erupted all over this country and across the entire world. Black people had had enough, and many allies also showed up to express their outrage at the police brutality that was pervasive in communities of color. It would be hard to believe that there was a dinner table in America that wasn't talking about the murder of George and race relations in general. Many white allies realized that the off-color remarks relatives made were actually racist and needed to be confronted. More than ever, they were trying to reach out to their racist family members who held long-standing prejudices against Black people and other people of color. Even within non-Black communities of color, allies were addressing the anti-Black sentiment that was present among their own people. This collective effort, for me, was really beautiful to see and hear about. It helped alleviate the feeling of being alone in trying to change hearts and minds.

This movement toward inclusivity was not met without resistance. Too many people were comfortable in their own ways of thinking. They didn't want to accept the messages highlighting oppression and inequality that were coming from the communities that were living it. Instead, they chose to arrogantly express their ignorance and claim authority on the experiences of others. One of the main ways that people were doing this was through social media. I saw debates, arguments, and outright fights breaking out in the comments sections of Instagram.

Ryan and I had long ago become inactive on Facebook, though we still had accounts. Facebook is the preferred social media platform for Ryan's parents, as well as many of his aunts and uncles. We didn't know it, but they were weighing in on everything from police brutality to systemic racism in general. Most of it wasn't pretty. It wasn't long before Jewel, Lucy, and others who disagreed with what Ryan's family was spewing reached out to Ryan himself.

"Are you going to say something?"

"Dude, your family is being racist. You have a Black wife and children; how are you staying silent?"

"You need to stand up for your wife and kids."

"You're the only one personally connected to this. People are waiting for you to say something."

This last comment surprised Ryan. It didn't make sense to him that people would care about his thoughts on this, but he gave it his consideration.

"Why do I need to go on Facebook and make a statement?" Ryan asked me one day. "I don't know, babe. It just seems disingenuous."

"I know," I replied. "But that's where the conversations are being held. They're being vile and going unchecked."

So Ryan logged on to his Facebook account for the first time in almost a decade and made a post:

> I haven't posted for eight years, but now seems like a
> good time. It's been a rough weekend in Omaha, and
> there are a lot of hurt people who I love and care for.

America hasn't healed from the sins of its past, and the wounds are still bleeding. Even if you don't believe you've helped cause the problem, you can still take ownership for your part of the solution. As a believer, I have a strong conviction that whoever wants to be a disciple of Jesus must deny themselves and take up their cross daily and follow him. I believe this means that we who believe need to take responsibility for the redemption of the world. Not just for our sins, but for the sins of our ancestors. Not just for your family, but for my family as well. Please do what you can so that my children won't have to fight the battles we ran away from.

Initially I was elated by Ryan's post. In plain view of everyone, he recognized racism was a problem that everyone needed to have a hand in dismantling. He acknowledged that our children would be touched by the failures of society if we didn't collectively work together. And he was doing it while using language that could speak directly to the hearts of many of the people he was connected to on Facebook—conservative Christians. We had arrived! He had found his voice! Relief washed over my body. But it wasn't long before the likes and comments came pouring in, and my optimism went flowing out.

I walked up to Ryan. "Babe, your post is problematic."

He turned to me, surprised. "Wait, what? How? What do you mean?"

"At first I really liked it, but have you gone back and looked at the comments?"

"No, I haven't."

I groaned and shook my head, not so much at Ryan, but more at what I was about to show him. I grabbed my phone and showed him some comments under his post. "Look. Look at this. You're getting praise. But look who it's coming from!"

Ryan was getting positive feedback, but it was from the very people who were justifying the killings of innocent Black men. They had attached themselves to his religious wording and were now thanking him for his wisdom while lamenting that "we need to do better." Messages of hope, nowhere to be found in their own posts, were popping up in Ryan's comments section. They hoped our children would grow up in a better world, even though "it is so hard to know what to do."

Ryan scanned the comments and scoffed at a few. "Wow, that's surprising coming from *her*."

"Exactly. Your post was convincing, but not confrontational."

A few days later, he made another post:

I've given a lot of thought to what's happened these past few days. A large part of the problem is that conservatives haven't taken on the responsibility to dismantle racism. It's been left to the liberals in our country. If anyone genuinely wants to solve racial inequality in this country, start by joining the movement that has been going on for decades. Like it or not, our institutions will be judged by our worst members, and if we don't take steps to fix that, we become complicit. I eagerly desire to see more conservatives not stay silent or only focus on the protests. Consider that if you become part of the solution, people will stop acting like you're the problem. There's a

Derek Chauvin in every church, business, and family.

If you don't think there is, it might be you.

The comments came pouring in, and this time they weren't too friendly. While there was some praise sprinkled in, this time Ryan's extended family came out of the woodwork with contrarian views. They promoted the words of Candace Owens, the Hodgetwins, and other Black voices who deny that racism exists. These voices have been weaponized to counteract and discredit the overwhelming number of Black and brown people with their own personal stories of experiencing racism. Arguments broke out in his comments section as Jewel and some of Ryan's friends and cousins showed up to offer their support. Other people, his own family members, showed up just to verbally attack and call him names.

I can't say I was too surprised by what I saw from Ryan's family, but I *was* surprised by how many people sat on the sidelines and said nothing. I wasn't surprised that so many of them refrained from engaging in discussions on race, but I was floored when no one stepped in when the bullying against Ryan and his sister started. Silence. Earsplitting silence. And to be clear, this entire family plays their lives out on Facebook. There was no way they didn't see these exchanges. Even when some of them were later confronted about their silence, none of them claimed to have not seen what was going on. So, yes, the silence spoke loudly. And no silence was more deafening than that of his mom and dad. They were nowhere to be found speaking up in defense of their own children. I was appalled. Ryan was, strangely and sadly, not surprised.

This time their silence was loaded. While Ryan knew that he had to have some very tough conversations with his parents, this wasn't something he jumped into. I had to fight my urge to be offended that he was taking his time to address this with his parents. It might have been easy to be mad, but when I took a moment to think about what this meant for him, I understood what was going on.

Ryan was afraid that if he confronted his parents, they would confirm that the image he had of them as loving and compassionate people was false. He faced the possibility that the parents he thought he knew were not those parents at all. The conversations could either lead to an assurance that they were the people who deep down he needed them to be; or it could lead to total heartache and mourning the loss of the parents he thought he had. Who was I to rush that moment for him?

But I would be lying if I said that I completely left the situation alone. I didn't have that much self-control. I did casually ask from time to time if he'd had a chance to talk to his parents.

Ryan had come to a point where he realized it was undeniable that his silence was contributing to a bigger picture. It kept him safe, but did damage to others. He was learning that silence is not synonymous with neutrality. With George Floyd's murder, he was finally able to comprehend the effects of sitting back and letting racism and prejudice go unchecked. When these attitudes are not met with resistance, we end up with police brutality in communities of color, white women shedding fake tears while calling the cops on people of color for simply going about their daily lives, and millions of children in this country sitting in classrooms receiving an education void of the BIPOC (Black, Indigenous, People of Color) narrative of our nation's history.

Ryan was not the only one experiencing a revelation about silence. I had my own silence to reckon with. No, I was not silent about the injustices going on in the public eye. I was, however, silent about my own experiences with racial discrimination. This was something I was socialized to do. I wasn't taught to not stand up for myself, but I was shown on a number of occasions that we, as Black people, could commiserate with one another, but we didn't necessarily talk about our hardships with white people.

I saw this when I witnessed different conversations between my parents and their friends. They could go deep with their Black friends without any subject being off-limits. Having a safe and understanding outlet, they discussed the hurtful comments from coworkers, the ignorance of a stranger in a store, or the umpteenth time they or someone they knew had to justify to a cop why they were in a certain space. There was a candidness that I didn't see or hear when my parents were hanging out with their white friends. This doesn't mean that they did not have genuine friendships with white people. They did. It just means that there was a part of their lives they didn't share with those friends. So, without receiving any explicit instructions that I can recall, I learned to navigate my relationships in the same way.

I can understand why my parents probably weren't sharing their racially charged experiences with their white friends. It's probably for the same reasons I chose not to. In some instances, white people just didn't want to hear it. "Why are you making it about race?" "Are you sure it wasn't about something else?" "I don't see color . . ." Those comments shut the conversation down right away.

Additionally, many white people are unaware how race plays a role in all things. To tell them about my experiences would mean that I had to assume the role of the teacher and explain to them why these things matter. To explain why these things matter is basically pleading for someone to care about your humanity as much as their own. That hurts, and I didn't have the emotional strength to bring that into those friendships where I hadn't perceived a hint of awareness on my white friends' part.

This isn't to say that I didn't have any white friends who were aware of the pervasiveness of racism in our society. I did. With those friends, I could talk about a few things, but I limited myself to only talking about the explicitly overt occurrences that were undeniably motivated by racist or prejudiced thoughts. I didn't want to touch on situations that required someone to understand what veiled racism felt like. Without them having those personal experiences themselves, I was in the exhausting role of teaching people what life looked like through my eyes. Like my parents, I became well-versed in code-switching and knowing with whom I could talk about certain subjects. Depending on the person, I knew what things were up for discussion and what was completely off-limits. It was the difference between a look of recognition and a look of doubt. It was the difference between a nod of affirmation and a headshake of skepticism. I could spot it immediately and it became second nature to move fluidly between people who got it and people who didn't.

After George's murder, I had my aha! moment regarding this methodical conversational chess game I was playing with each of my social groups. It happened when I received a text message from one of my white friends. She wasn't someone in my inner circle, but she was someone I trusted. We were moving in the direction of building a close friendship and she hadn't give me any reason to believe I couldn't be myself around her. When my phone buzzed and her name popped up with a message, I smiled. And then, I started reading. My smile faded.

> Hey! Can you explain to me this whole Black Lives Matter movement? I don't know what it's all about, and I thought you would be the perfect resource to help me get started in understanding it! I am kind of confused because none of the people of color in my

circle have faced discrimination. So what can you tell
me about this? Thanks!

I was taken aback by this message. My jaw dropped, and my heart
sank. I read it over and over again. The casual way in which she referred to me as a resource was disarming. It was clear that she didn't
understand what it was she was asking of me. I was caught off guard by
both the huge ask and her honest lack of knowledge on the topic. To
be completely transparent, I sobbed. My phone started ringing, and I
saw that it was Jewel. In a haze of sorts, I answered the call, but when
I opened my mouth to greet her, nothing came out. I couldn't calm
myself down enough to even say "Hello." In the silence, she spoke.

"Jenn? Hello?"

It was then that I gasped, not even realizing that I was holding my
breath.

"Oh my gosh, Jenn! Are you OK?"

"No. No, I'm not," I sobbed.

"What's going on?"

I read the text to her, choking back the newly formed tears that
came at reading it once again.

"I can't believe she would put that on you. She needs to do the work
herself. It's not your job to educate her."

"Yes! Thank you! I just can't believe it. How could she possibly say
that people of color don't experience discrimination?"

That text sat unanswered for several days. And unfortunately, hers
was not the only one of its nature to come to me in that season of
protests in defense of Black lives. While they were all problematic in
some way, this original text sat heaviest in my heart because of one line:
"None of the people of color in my circle have faced discrimination."

I sat with that and replayed it over and over again in my mind. I vacillated between bewilderment and anger. And then one day, as I sat stewing over what she'd said, it dawned on me with such clarity. She didn't know we faced discrimination because none of us shared this part of our lives with her. With that in mind, I was able to calm down and respond.

> Hey, I needed some time to gather my thoughts. If you think the people of color in your circle haven't faced discrimination, it's only because we haven't discussed it with you. I assure you, we have all (in some form or fashion) been touched by it. I am faced with it every time I leave my house. Right now, I'm struggling because I'm having to hold things together by day because I want to spare my children the generational trauma that comes from being a person of color in this country. I know your request seems simple, but I have to point you to resources because the act of walking through the initial steps with you is literally asking me to continually sit in my racial pain. I can handle questions and conversations centered around specific issues, but to tackle the topic in general is something I cannot do out of my need for self-preservation.

As hurtful as it was to receive that text (in which she was genuinely asking for help to understand), I will forever be grateful that she took the step to reach out. With one text I realized what my silence was doing to the Black community, as well as to my entire social circle. I thought I was wisely navigating social circles by choosing what to say to some and what to keep from others. But with one text, I came to understand that my silence was allowing people like my friend to see and hear about things in the national dialogue and think to themselves, *Well, I have Black friends and friends of color, and they don't experience that.* It allowed people to distance themselves from racism and, consequently, from having to think about whether or not they are part of the problem or the solution.

It takes more than love to find your voice and use it

You can love someone, or an entire community, and still unknowingly work against what they are trying to achieve by sitting on the sidelines in the midst of their struggles. That's what Ryan had done. Every time he didn't speak up, he was planting seeds of doubt in my mind as to how he felt about certain issues that directly affected me. I began to doubt whether or not he felt anything at all. Even worse, there were times when I thought he may actually agree with words or acts that I felt were oppressive.

Even after he had his individual reckoning that brought him to a place of empathy, it still wasn't clear to him that he needed to use his voice. It took someone explicitly pointing out that his silence was, in fact, sending a message. And it was a message he did not want to be sending.

As for me, my silence was hurting my brothers and sisters of all races who were standing up and speaking out against discrimination.

I was not verbally invalidating their experiences, but my silence was. I wasn't lending my support. I wasn't giving people within my sphere of influence a brown face to personalize the message of discrimination. A brown face. This brown face. My brown face.

Moving forward, I decided that I would no longer censor myself. I would wade past my own discomfort. I would not worry about whether or not I said everything perfectly. I would stop caring if what I had to say made other people uncomfortable. If I wanted to speak up, no one was going to shut me down. The repercussions of silence were just too strong.

Chapter 17

The Path Isn't Always Straight

I learned a lot about both Ryan and myself as I watched him take his journey to becoming anti-racist. I felt relieved as I heard Ryan describe different situations with a newfound compassion. He also took initiative in seeking out information in different sectors where he felt he could personally make an impact. He became interested in finding out who was a watchdog for the local police department; he started asking me questions about the curriculum being taught in schools and if things were taught from more than just a white perspective. He started researching the history of racial tension in Omaha.

To see him coming into his own and taking ownership of his place within the anti-racist movement lifted a weight off my shoulders. I didn't have to plead for him to recognize his role in improving how race impacted the way our children and I had to move through society. He was being transformed into a person who I could count on as a partner in doing this work.

The impetus for finally having a conversation with his mom came after receiving video links from her of Black conservatives who were belittling and denouncing the protests breaking out all over the world in support of Black lives. She never once asked her son how his Black wife was feeling about everything going on. She never once asked him how the current events might be affecting his household. No. She went straight to sending him her stance on the state of race relations by finding the few voices that allowed her to stay comfortable and dismiss racism as an actual problem.

Ryan walked away from that two-hour conversation completely deflated.

"How did the conversation go, babe?"

"My mom basically confirmed my fears about who she is. She isn't interested in learning about opinions that are different than her own. I'm afraid that she is going to grow old and bitter until she has isolated herself from her entire family."

I wasn't surprised that it went the way it did, though I was surprised how deeply Ryan's sadness ran.

"I'm so sorry." My voice was reduced to a whisper.

"She wouldn't listen to a word I said. She tried to throw it back on you. She blamed you for avoiding her. I told her that you don't behave that way with any other person on this planet, and *that* should say something. She didn't want to hear it."

I saw the heartbreak written all over his face. A little piece of his hope had been extinguished by how his mom showed up in the conversation.

A few days later, Ryan talked to his dad, and that conversation faired a bit better.

"My dad actually wept on the phone. I haven't heard him cry like that before."

"Wow," I said, surprised. "What did he say?"

"He is devastated about how fractured his family has become, and he's not sure what to do next."

"What did he say when you talked to him specifically about race?"

"He's confused. He doesn't understand. He said that growing up, he was taught to not see race. The goal of the '60s and '70s was to move beyond race and to see one another as human. He's disappointed to realize that what he was taught might not be good enough anymore."

"It's taking everything in me not to roll my eyes at that, but I get that he's being genuine."

"I know. He doesn't get it. But he's open, and I think this is an opportunity for us to have some continued conversations about this. I've always wanted more of a relationship with my dad. I think we have to leave my mom out of this. I'm not going to waste my time talking to her right now. I'm going to focus on my dad."

And just like that, Ryan's hope was ignited a little bit that counteracted the despair he felt as a result of his conversation with his mom.

For several days, Ryan stewed over his parents' starkly different reactions to his having initiated honest conversations about race. He knew things couldn't continue as they always had. Not because I had finally gotten through to him, but because he was finally understanding how damaging the status quo really was.

"My parents have to do better. They have got to move on this issue. I don't think they are trying to intentionally hurt you, but whether they know it or not, they are triggering you and could potentially trigger the kids in the future. I need to see forward movement from them, and I am going to hold them accountable."

Yes, yes, yes! The protector who I had been yearning for was finally making an appearance. Ryan had been giving his parents a pass because he felt they didn't realize how their actions and words were affecting me. But finally, *finally*, Ryan realized that impact far outweighs intent. Good intentions don't undo the harm done.

Too many people shrug off the hurt they cause others because they hide behind the excuse of having good intentions or being unaware that they were causing harm. They use that reasoning to justify not acknowledging the hurt, and that leads to and perpetuates fractured relationships. Ryan now saw this clearly. It didn't matter that his parents didn't know what they were doing or didn't mean to hurt me with their words. What mattered most was the effect their behaviors were having on me, as well as the potential effect they could have on our kids.

Over the next couple of weeks, the walls around the racially traumatized parts of my heart slowly came down. I started sharing experiences with Ryan that I had never told him, previously fearful that my vulnerability would be met with a distant sympathy, indifference, or him playing devil's advocate. I felt more comfortable being my whole self and felt free to point out oppressive subtexts in things we read or watched without fear that he would tire of it. I grew secure in the path that Ryan and I were on.

I was growing ever more comfortable with and grateful for our COVID-19-induced isolation that allowed us to grow and heal together. I felt like nothing could rock our boat. I was quickly proven wrong when Ryan approached me one morning as I was savoring a cup of coffee outside, enjoying the breeze.

"Hey babe, I'm thinking about taking a trip up north to see my parents. What do you think?"

"Wait, what? Are you serious?"

"Yeah. I haven't seen them in several months. And I want to take the kids with me. They keep saying they miss Grandma and Grandpa. And I miss my parents."

"You want to take the kids up to Fargo? Right now? I disagree with that one hundred percent. I can't even believe you're suggesting this."

"OK, but why?"

I looked at him in disbelief. "Why? Are you serious right now? For one, there's a pandemic going on! It's actually physically not safe. And two, your parents are not emotionally safe for our kids to be around."

"We will be going from our door to their door. I'll only stop once for gas."

"And when the kids have to go to the bathroom?"

"I'll bring the little potty. We'll stop on the side of the road. They won't see the inside of a gas station or a rest stop."

"I can't believe this. And when is it that you're wanting to go?"

He took out his phone and opened up his calendar app. "Second or third week of July."

I shook my head and scoffed. "Well, I don't even know why you're talking to me about this. Your mind is already made up. I don't really have a say."

He looked at me and sighed. "Don't say that. You always have a say in this."

I decided to put that to the test. "Then no. Don't go."

"Jenn, I'd really like to."

I shook my head indignantly. "Well, fine. Go. But you're not taking my kids up there. Go if you have to. But don't you come back and get us all sick with COVID!"

"Is this really about COVID, or is it about me going to see my parents?"

During the next several days, we had different versions of the same argument. Ryan was stating his case, I was stating mine, and neither of us was interested in what the other had to say.

"I can't believe you're going to reward your parents' behavior by taking our kids up to see them."

"I'm not rewarding them with anything. I want to go visit my parents. I will have some tough conversations while I'm there. But I know the kids miss their grandparents."

"Your mom is toxic. She is harmful. She is actually resisting learning anything about the struggles of the Black community—a community her grandkids are a part of!"

"My dad is trying."

"Because he's read a couple of chapters of *White Like Me*? And what growth have you seen come from that? He hasn't even had time to show any growth!"

Honestly, it felt like a sucker punch to the gut. That might sound extreme, but it really did take the air right out of my lungs. *What happened to his resolve that his parents needed to do the work of learning about the ramifications of present-day racism? What happened to holding them accountable to a commitment to doing better?* That wall around my heart? Yeah, that started creeping back up. I was confused. It seemed like his actions were not aligning with his words and that my feelings were unimportant to him.

Before COVID-19, we had found a good compromise in Ryan going to Fargo with the kids every few months while I stayed behind for a Mommy Weekend. But Ryan knew that I still felt a twinge of tension every time they went. If I felt so strongly that I needed to stay home to guard my heart, what did it mean that I was willing to send my kids? I usually pacified this nagging thought of mine by telling myself that my kids were still too young to read into the things his parents said and did. But now they were getting older—and now, in 2020, it was plain as day: they couldn't be counted on to keep my kids safe.

My emotions were running high. Forget trying to communicate logically with him. For all the progress Ryan and I had made, this felt like a huge step in the wrong direction. Since starting the therapy process, we had been able to talk through anything. We worked really hard at acknowledging what the other felt and committing ourselves to working through issues, even if we had to table conversations for another time. This was the first time in a long time that we felt stuck. Of course, I turned to Sophia.

"I can't believe he wants to go to Fargo. I thought he was starting to get it," I lamented with my head in my hands.

Thank God for Sophia. With kind, understanding eyes, she looked at me for several seconds before speaking.

"I get that you don't want him to go. I think he's crazy for wanting to take four kids up to North Dakota during a pandemic. But as far as wanting to see his parents, you need to cut him some slack."

"What? Are you seri—"

"Tell me again why you changed high schools after ninth grade."

I gave her a puzzled look. I didn't get what this had to do with anything, but I answered her question anyway. "Because I was tired of being one of the only kids of color in the school. I just couldn't do it anymore."

"OK. And how did you feel once you got to your new, more diverse high school?"

"Relieved. There was so much diversity. Lots of other Black students."

"But what happened once you really got to know some of them?"

I sighed. "I realized that I didn't fit in as much as I had hoped I would. I didn't have the same interests, the same childhood references. I couldn't completely relate to them either. I felt alone because I didn't know anyone else in that situation."

Sophia let a silence fall over us before she spoke again. "Think about this. Ryan is realizing that his perspective and some of his core values are diverging from those of his parents. He is on a journey to a life of prioritizing and exercising anti-racism. But all around him are people either like his parents, who are wondering what all the fuss is about, or people like you, who are urging him to be ten steps ahead of where he actually is."

"He's in between two worlds," I said quietly as it all began to become clear to me.

She nodded and lowered her voice to match mine. "He's in between two worlds. Who in his life understands exactly what he's dealing with?"

"No one."

"He's not going up there to reward his parents. He's going up there, equipped with his new understanding, hoping that he might finally be able to help his parents change their hearts."

I chewed on that conversation with Sophia in the following days. I realized that there was truth to what she had said. Ryan had been able to learn and unlearn some very important lessons. He was optimistic that, with his guidance, his parents might be able to make the shift as well. He wanted to take this trip to see them to take on the tough conversations in hopes that they would hear him and reconsider their positions on things. Once passive and generalizing, he was prepared to be specific, to push for change, and to explain that their relationship with us and our children would change if they didn't reckon with some of their attitudes.

I finally recognized that it wasn't my job to encourage or discourage Ryan's efforts to get through to his parents about the importance of this moment we were living in. It didn't matter whether or not I believed that they could suspend their beliefs about society long enough to see how life is for non-white people and how they, as white people, should care enough about equity to try to do their part in moving things forward in their own communities. Only they could show him, with their words and actions, if his optimism was unfounded or not. I was veering out of my lane. This was between Ryan and his parents, and once I figured that out, I was content to let Ryan discover on his own whether or not his parents were capable of change.

In gaining a better perspective on these things, I knew that I could best support him by showing him I believed in him. I came to accept the visit to see his parents and was able to send him and our children off with my blessing. He hoped to elicit change in his family, and it was a hope that I didn't want to extinguish. While it was unlikely that everything (if anything) would be resolved during this one trip, I was rooting for him. And that meant that, ultimately, I had to root for his parents.

It takes more than love to walk alongside someone on their journey of change

While it appeared that Ryan was taking backward steps in his journey of anti-racism, he had not regressed. Ryan was trudging forward and encountering new circumstances or thoughts that forced him to re-assess before moving forward again. While frustrated in the moment, I had to be honest with myself. *Did I want him to keep moving forward with doubt in his mind? What would the result of that look like?* If he had to take a minute to process, ask questions, and dig deeper only to be able to move forward with more conviction in his heart than before, then so be it!

I wanted Ryan to be able to defend a stance of anti-racism until he was blue in the face. I wanted him to believe it in the depths of his heart so that his resolve would be unshakable. To do that, he had to go through this process, this journey. *His* process, *his* journey. That's when I really learned that the path to anti-racism (or any journey, really) is not a straight line. It has twists and turns and sometimes appears to double back. These "detours" aren't actually detours. They are all part of the journey.

I still had to deal with my hurt feelings. Once I realized why I was taking things so personally, the sting lessened. I was centering myself in his journey. I was making a correlation between his progress in pushing back on racism and his love for me. This was unfair, unhealthy, and untrue. His inability to immediately grasp all of the tenets of anti-racism did not mean that his love for me wasn't real, strong, and ever-growing. I just needed to breathe, engage in self-care, and stop centering myself in a path that only he could walk. My husband was earnest in learning and growing, and I needed to trust in that.

This is a lesson that extends to the broader context of any journey that I am privileged enough to witness. I don't need to see the journey through my lens. I need to have the humility to step back and allow space for the process to take place. I would hope that Ryan (or anyone else, for that matter) would give me the same courtesy.

Ryan's eventual trip up north with the kids left him brokenhearted. He didn't want to give me too many details about what anyone said. He just said one thing: "I think it's going to a long while before we go back up there."

And it was. It would be another year before he saw them again.

Having seen and heard his parents' apathy and unwillingness to learn, Ryan has shown up as the protector of our kids. He has stepped in to correct and shut down anything unproductive from his parents.

It hasn't been comfortable for him, but that is a tension that he now has to straddle as he maintains his relationship with his family while keeping our kids safe.

Chapter 18

Bringing Our Kids on the Journey

After George Floyd was murdered, it was hard to look at my kids and pretend that the world was something it wasn't. I knew that I had to start talking to my children about race in a way that went beyond saying that God had created all people with a spectrum of beautiful skin colors. We had to get real about race and how it affected people's daily lives. With them being eight, seven, five, and three, I decided to take one approach with my oldest daughter and son and another approach with my two youngest girls.

Books are a powerful teaching tool for children of any age, in and out of the classroom. With my little girls, I ramped up my efforts to bring books into our home that had characters who represented a variety of ethnicities, language groups, socioeconomic statuses, physical ability levels, sexual orientations, and gender identities. I wanted them to become comfortable seeing people from all walks of life in the stories we read. My goal was to the lay the groundwork for more explicit conversations down the road by normalizing images and stories of people from varied backgrounds now.

The images and stories my girls heard provided opportunities for me to hear what their preconceived notions were (yes, even at young ages they had assumptions about how the world should work) and to gently invite them to be open to other ways of experiencing the world.

"Mommy, that boy is wearing a dress! Boys can't wear dresses!"

"They can if they want. This boy isn't bothering anyone by wearing a dress. And girls can wear business suits, like this one here."

With my older kids, our work involved having more explicit conversations about race. I knew that, unlike the experience I'd had in school, I did not want to approach conversations about being Black by only talking about slavery and segregation. I found two amazing books that focused on telling the triumphant stories of Black men and women in all fields and of all talents. Each night, we talked about one man and one woman. The stories of their triumphs inevitably led us to discuss and unpack some pretty big terms. We talked about segregation, racism, abolition, white supremacy, and bias to name a few.

In the beginning, I felt sad to have to open my kids' eyes to these ideas. It was a feeling, I assumed, that many parents of color have had when they felt compelled to have these talks with their kids.

One night, I talked to Ryan about how I was feeling. "It breaks my heart to have to talk to them about this. I knew it was coming, but it just feels like taking a piece of their childhood away."

"It's something we need to do," he said. "And on the nights that I'm home, I'll be right there with you to do it."

And he was. Ryan didn't position himself as an authority on what we were talking about. But he was the perfect wingman, with Google images and YouTube at the ready to show the kids real pictures and videos about the people we were learning about that night.

My sadness was soon replaced with comfort as these conversations became more natural. The kids were very engaged in our discussions and asked a lot of really good questions. They asked about the meaning behind Jim Crow and why enslaved people had the same last name as their enslavers.

Reading about the different people allowed us to start piecing different parts of history together. The kids began to learn the importance of historical context. Knowing the culture of the country during a person's lifetime helped them to understand the challenges they faced and some of the decisions they made. When I read about someone, we always learned about the year of their birth and the year of their death, and the kids would speculate aloud about what was going on in the U.S. at that time.

"OK, that means they were probably born into slavery."

"*Circa* means they don't really know when they were born."

"That was during the Civil War."

"Segregation was still the law."

As a teacher and a mom, it warmed my heart. They often didn't want our nightly reading time to end, and neither did I.

I discovered one major blind spot arising from opening up the conversation about race by focusing on people who had made history for fighting back against racism. Even though many of the figures in the books were still alive today, it became clear to me that the kids were treating our talks about race, and the numerous barriers that people had broken, as a history lesson. They were not connecting what we were talking about to present times or even their own reality.

"It's a good thing all those people are dead," my daughter said to me one time.

"They aren't."

Shock swept across their little faces. "They're not?"

"You know how I told you that Mimi and Granddad went to segregated schools?"

They nodded.

"Well, Mimi and Granddad are still alive, which means that some of the people who thought segregation was good are still alive too," I said.

The kids sat there chewing on that for a moment. Then I continued. "And just like Mimi and Granddad had kids and passed down the lesson of loving everyone, those people had kids too. And a lot of them probably didn't pass down messages of loving everyone. You might come across some people who are my age or even your age who think it's OK to not treat people nicely just because of how we look."

Another blind spot of mine surfaced one night as we were reading. My sweet son, a real feeler, looked at me with a crushing innocence.

"Mom, why do they [white people] always treat us like this?"

That question nearly knocked the breath out of me. "Oh buddy, it's not everyone, and they don't always treat us like this."

Of course he thought this. Many of the people we were learning about were oppressed under slavery and Jim Crow laws, which started a repetitive narrative of white people being oppressors. I had unintentionally done what I said I wouldn't do. No, I didn't use slavery or segregation as a springboard into these conversations. But many of the heroes we read about had to contend with slavery and/or segregation, so it was present in our conversations even though it wasn't the focus. Even when we read about contemporary figures who were breaking barriers to become the first Black person to achieve a new height, it highlighted preferential treatment for and a normalization of being white.

I knew I needed to pivot and take our talks in a new direction. "I want to talk about allies. Do you know what it means to be an ally?"

They shook their heads.

"Well, when you're an ally, it means that you use your privilege to stand with those who don't have that same privilege, and you get in the fight with them. There are white allies. Like Daddy."

I went on to name other people in our friend group who were allies. I wanted the kids to know that we had allies all around us. That made my son feel better.

"And while we call on our allies to stand with us, it's important for us to be allies to others."

My daughter chimed in. "But Mommy, we're Black. We can't be allies."

"Oh, we can absolutely be allies! We may not have the privilege of a preferred skin color, but you have plenty of other privileges that can make you an ally for others."

"Like what?"

"Well, you have two parents who live with you. Some kids are treated differently because they don't have that. You have a mom and a dad. Some kids who have two moms or two dads are treated differently. You have full usage of your entire body. You don't ever have to worry about not being able to move around in a building that may not have a ramp or elevator."

I went on to name other privileges they had and explained how kids and adults without those privileges might come up against roadblocks while just trying to live.

"You don't have to feel guilty about your privileges, but we are called to step up and join in the fight when someone isn't being treated right for not having those privileges. You can be an ally right now, as a kid."

"How?"

"Your names are easy to pronounce, but you go to school with lots of kids whose names are not common in English. Many kids will be too afraid to tell an adult when they are mispronouncing their name. If you ever see that, you can say, 'That's not how you say his or her or their name.' Then tell them how it's correctly pronounced."

"Sometimes when we have a sub, they don't say my friends' names right," my daughter said.

"Exactly. A person's name is important and needs to be pronounced correctly every time. Or there are people who are treated as not smart because they don't speak English very well. And some people can get really angry when they try to talk to someone and figure out that English isn't their first language. You two are bilingual. Step in and ask if you can help translate. You see Mommy do this all the time."

My conversations with the kids reinforced a belief that I'd instinctively had all along: the minds of young people are very capable of grasping profound concepts. Though tempting, I never wanted to overstep and make decisions for them. My job as their parent was to equip them with the critical lens that would enable them to make the best choices they could for themselves. That was never clearer to me than on the eve of the Fourth of July when my husband and I sat to discuss the upcoming holiday with our older two.

"So what holiday is tomorrow?"

"The Fourth of July!" they screamed excitedly.

"Yes. And what are we celebrating on the Fourth of July?"

"Freedom!"

"OK. Freedom was declared in 1776. So, was everyone free?"

"No! There were still slaves back then."

"Right. We might hear people talk about the Fourth of July being a celebration of freedom, but it's important to know that we are talking about this country's freedom from British rule, not necessarily freedom for all people."

"But now all people are free, right?"

"Well, we still have work to do so that all people have all freedoms. That's why it's so important to be an ally for people who are still fighting for equality."

"Who is still fighting for equality?"

"Well, in some places, Jewel and Lucy could still lose their jobs just because they are married. It's important for us to be allies for them. No one should be treated like that."

"Are Grandma and Grandpa allies for them?" my daughter asked.

And there it was. Our conversations about anti-racism and inclusion were converging with our lives. Grandma and Grandpa are the names the kids use to refer to Ryan's parents. I looked at Ryan, then looked back at my daughter.

"You know what? You never have to ask if someone is an ally. You can listen to their words and, more importantly, watch their actions."

"OK, Mommy," was all she said.

That response saved me from having to tell her that her grandparents were not allies to the LGBTQIA+ community, and it drove home the importance of paying attention to what the people around you are saying and doing. It's not my job to break my children's hearts. That burden lies with Ryan's parents.

The kids and I had these intentional conversations all summer long and well into the fall. Eventually we reached a point where it became commonplace and natural to have talks about injustice. Halfway through the summer, I realized that I had not put my healing work on hold at all. The work I was doing with my kids was part of my own healing journey. I couldn't go back and change the hurtful experiences I'd had as a kid that had left me shocked and without words. But I could be the support for my kids that I wish I'd had. I've come to see the work that I do with my kids regarding race as some of the most important work I will ever do in my life.

It takes more than love to raise children who understand the importance of inclusion and fighting racism

I was sad that I had to open my kids' eyes to the realities that fueled our conversations that summer. But I knew that my sadness at opening their eyes to injustices in the world would pale in comparison to the sadness I would feel had they been blindsided by ignorance and racism without any warning that things like this existed. I was more saddened by the knowledge that there were families who didn't shoulder the burden of discussing race and oppression with their children and that these children could grow up to be some of our biggest offenders because of that.

Telling my kids to be nice and calling it a day was not an option. Children need explicit examples of what different behaviors look like (both the desired and undesired ones). We role-played different situations and actually practiced identifying different situations as racist and saying, "That's racist." Those are big words, and we talked at length about the weight of such words. We went through numerous situations in which they could come to someone else's defense, along with when it was safe to defend someone on their own and when it was best to go get an adult.

Like any other human, my kids aren't always going to get it right. Try as I might, being confronted with instances of racism and discrimination is jarring and will likely result in them being shocked into silence sometimes. But I've seen evidence in my classroom and at home that, after modeling for kids how to advocate for themselves and giving them the language to navigate a situation, children will use their words.

Every parent wants to build upon what they were given by their parents and give their kids even more. I was having conversations about race and oppression with my kids in an effort to provide them with a type of support that I wish I'd had growing up.

My childhood was in no way lacking. I had parents who supported me even to the point where it didn't make sense. They were and continue to be my cheerleaders in everything, and that kind of unconditional love from parental figures is something that many people (including my husband) can only dream of.

But when my parents were raising my brothers and me, their priority was to give us access. Access to everything. They grew up in a time when segregation was law; they were literally cut off from resources in every sector of their lives.

They vowed that their children would have access to everything they needed and most of what they wanted. They made a decision to move out of a part of Omaha that was primarily Black because just being from there gives people certain ideas about what kind of person you are. They worked hard and reached a financial freedom that neither side of my family tree had ever experienced, enabling us to participate in any and every extracurricular activity. And though they raised us to believe we would foot the bill for whatever college we chose, when it came time to go, we had the choice to go anywhere without them so much as mentioning the cost.

Access was something they didn't have, and they made it their goal to give that to their kids. With that in mind, they didn't anticipate some of the struggles that would stem from raising us in white spaces as the only children of color. I can't blame them. I don't blame them. They were protecting me from the pain of *their* youth, much like I'm attempting to protect my children from the pain of *my* youth. And one day I'm sure my kids will clue me in on the things that I'm missing, try as I might to anticipate their struggles.

Chapter 19

Personal Steps Toward Healing

For the entirety of that summer, my therapy sessions were all online due to COVID-19. While there was an option to do Eye Movement Desensitization Reprocessing (EMDR) virtually to start working through racial trauma, I opted to wait until we could meet in person. Sophia and I were still able to have really productive sessions in which she helped me navigate conversations with Ryan and my reactions to the hurtful response of his family to the outcry against police brutality and systemic racism.

I spent a lot of time reflecting on my marriage and how we ended up in crisis because we didn't know how to navigate the dynamic of race. I also watched Ryan as he went through his journey of setting boundaries with and speaking up to his parents. After having the time and space to really think back on our journey as a married couple and to consider the possible ways we could have avoided the near-ruin of our marriage, I took stock of the lessons I was learning. Oh, how I wished I had known someone who could have given me some direction in terms of the conversations Ryan and I needed to be having during those early days. I felt compelled to speak out about it. I couldn't be the only person in this situation. If I was experiencing this, there had to be others. My mind was a flurry of thoughts.

I vacillated between creating a blog and writing a book. Ultimately, I ended up doing both. The initial idea of a blog became an Instagram account: @takesmorethanlove. I have Sophia to thank for that name. In one of our early sessions, I broke down, wondering how I ended up with a man who didn't understand race—something so fundamental to my everyday experiences. As I sat there sobbing, she said something I'll never forget: "You fell in love, honey, and it's gotten you this far. But it's going to take more than love to keep you going."

The IG posts allowed me to begin talking about ideas that would eventually become this memoir. While my initial motivation was to be a supportive voice to let people know that they weren't alone in this journey, the process of posting on IG and writing this book became cathartic. Posting and conversing in the comments section allowed me to fine-tune my thoughts, perspectives, and word choices when it came to discussing race.

Soon, the discussions moved from online to in real life. Immediately after George Floyd was murdered, many educators who had long been invested in Anti-bias, Anti-racist (ABAR) teaching practices facilitated webinars and Zoom conferences. It's very possible that these learning opportunities were offered before everyone was sheltered in place due to COVID-19, but I became aware of and started engaging in these talks during my months at home. My wheels were turning about how to help transform my school to become an ABAR school community.

As it turned out, four colleagues at my school were also diving into these talks and their wheels were turning as well. We eventually found ourselves in a Zoom meeting together and made plans to virtually debrief afterward. While we debriefed, we went through all of the amazing quotes we walked away with and dreamed aloud of the things our school could do to center our students and their families. Toward the end of the call, someone finally vocalized what we were all thinking and wishing.

"Guys, I think we just formed our school's ABAR committee."

We reached out to our principal, who eagerly jumped on board. We started our journey to creating a school in which the staff collaborated with students and families to make sure they felt seen and heard as an important part of our school community. We began the work of examining if our lessons and school-wide policies and procedures reflected our belief that every single individual is valued. This will be a journey that never ends, and I'm so grateful to be working with teachers who seek justice for any students who feels "othered" in some form or fashion.

School wasn't the only place where I started to use my voice. Throughout the entire summer, our church faithfully sent out weekly newsletters about the goings-on within the congregation—who was sick, pregnant, engaged, or newly married, different virtual conferences, and other announcements. Week after week I scoured the newsletter, only to be disappointed by the absence of anything concerning the civil unrest over the killings of unarmed Black folks.

I've often felt that, though they want to be influential in their communities, churches are too slow to enter into productive conversations about what is going on in society. Not being very engaged with our leadership, I reached out to members of our congregation who did have relationships with some of our elders to see if any conversations were being had. I learned that some white members had already spoken up about the fact that the elders weren't saying anything. I also learned that some of our church leadership had had some conversations with other members of color about race. But in the end, our church still had not put out a unified statement about where they stood.

I was furious. After weeks of not seeing anything from our church leadership, I'd had enough. "Ryan, what the heck, man? Why isn't our church saying anything?"

"I don't know. I really don't know."

"I'm furious. I just want to walk away. How can we be part of a church that ignores human suffering?"

"We can't walk away just yet. It's worth saying something. And then, if we feel like the elders are unresponsive, we can have a conversation about finding a new place to worship."

Maybe he had a point. I supposed it *was* possible to be that unaware. I took the leap and wrote to my all-white, all-male church leadership about my concerns over our church not being anti-racist in their practices and having work to do in the area of being trauma-informed.

> Good morning,
>
> I'm writing to inquire as to why our church has not engaged in the national dialogue that is taking place on race. I've been waiting and waiting to hear acknowledgment and support from the leaders of my faith community, and it has been met with silence. I am aware that some conversations have been had with leadership by allies and by some of our members of color that have scratched the surface of what is going on in communities of color. I just need to make sure that everyone knows that silence does not equal neutrality. To remain silent on an issue is to take a stance, and the silence is deafening.
>
> Part of my struggle in writing this email is that I don't have a personal relationship with any of you. I don't like that my first communication with you is of this

nature. Normally, I don't like to point out shortcomings unless I have a history of building you up first. But we've come to the point where I have to be true to myself and speak up.

Be well.

That initial email turned into more. Those emails led to large socially-distanced discussion panels led by members of color as well as our allies. Those led to small group conversations about how to make meaningful changes. I felt encouraged by the direction it started to take.

There were people in the congregation who were not excited about these conversations. Many questioned why we were having them. One wolf in sheep's clothing deceived a friend of mine into thinking she was worried about me and asked for my phone number. She wasn't worried about me; she only obtained my number to tell me how Satan was using me and others like me to divide our church. Ultimately, the noise from the opposition grew too loud and the leadership ceased any and all movement in the direction of discussing racial reconciliation as it pertains to a faith community.

But the damage was done. I had seen the real opinions of people I had worshipped next to for years. People that I had entrusted with my children's edification in our faith were the same ones not giving a damn about Black lives. It was scary and heartbreaking all at once. Ryan was seeing it too. My mind was made up. I wasn't going to go back. I wasn't so sure about Ryan, who was more attached to our church community. I needed to know where he stood. I asked him point-blank, "What are we going to do when people start meeting in person?"

He looked me dead in the eye. "We aren't going back to that place. It's not safe for you. It's not safe for the kids." Relief flooded my soul.

A year later, Ryan took me to a church that he was sure I was going to like. He had been once before, by himself, to scout it out. There were multiracial families everywhere. Even the pastoral team was multiracial—it felt like paradise—it felt like the Kingdom. At one point during the sermon, the white pastor was reading scriptures about unity and giving modern-day examples of how to show up for others in unity. His examples were numerous.

"That means," he started, "we stand with our Black and brown brothers when they are being oppressed."

I couldn't believe my ears. Tears started to fall. Ryan leaned over and whispered jokingly into my ear, "I think he knew you would be here today." We went back the next Sunday. And the next. We've been going back ever since.

I will say one thing for now: If you're noticing that this work needs to be done at your church and you're coming up against resistance, it's not Jesus you need to re-examine. It's your fellow churchgoers. Stay in the fight as long as you can, with compassion. Bow out if and when you need to. There's wisdom in knowing when a fight is not your fight and making the decision to walk away for your own emotional and spiritual health.

It takes more than love to know what healing looks like

I don't share these different things I did as a way to say "Look at me! I was making change!" I share them because, as you may have already noticed, they have a theme. I was honoring my painful experiences and giving them a voice. Whether it was conversations with my kids, sharing lessons I had learned on social media, or trying to create change in the institutions where I spent most of my time, I was no longer pushing my pain below the surface. When I saw a place for my voice to create awareness and potential change, I didn't shy away from it.

It went deeper than just acting in the moment. For so long I had lost my voice. I had opted for silence in the face of opposition. Silence was as much a part of my racial trauma as the actual events that produced the trauma. I would never be able to return to the past and speak in the moments when I had regretfully stayed silent. But by seeking out and engaging in opportunities to speak about my pain as a means of creating change, I discovered that I was counteracting the silence of the past that had dominated and perpetuated my racial trauma. Old wounds can be tended to and healed through our actions of the present.

Silence would no longer hold me captive to my racial trauma—it would now fuel my action. Gone were the days when I would be silent.

Chapter 20

Bringing It All to the Surface

I was overjoyed when Sophia reopened her office doors to her clients who were waiting to do EMDR. I was eager but nervous at the same time. Though I had heard nothing but positive things about EMDR therapy, I was nervous that my hurts were far too deep, far too painful, for anything to have an impact.

"OK, so we're going to start off with something I call floating."

I gave her a blank stare. "OK. What does that mean exactly?"

"I know your most recent trigger is the blow-up from last Christmas, but in talking to you, I know there are things that happened well before Ryan's family came into the picture that contribute to your racial trauma."

I nodded slowly. She wasn't wrong.

Sophia handed me two little oval-shaped green objects that were joined by a thick black cable that ran to a small box with dials on it that she held in her own hands. As I placed one oval in each palm and closed my hands over them, she twisted the dial and each object started to buzz at alternating times. It was mesmerizing.

Left hand buzz.

Right hand buzz.

Left hand buzz.

Right hand buzz.

Without me willing them to do so, my eyes followed suit. When the left hand buzzed, my eyes darted left. When the right hand buzzed, my eyes darted right. Back and forth. Back and forth.

"Just keep breathing," she said. "I'm going to start you off by directing you to think about a certain time in your life, and you're going to let your mind wander. During certain points in the process, I will ask you to tell me what you see or hear. It might be totally random. It doesn't matter. Just tell me what you're noticing."

What Sophia was doing was an unrestricted form of EMDR, allowing all of my unprocessed memories to come to the surface. As my mind wandered, what seemed like random occurrences came flowing out of my mouth.

Sophia asked, "What are you seeing right now?"

"There was this time I was at a cheerleading competition in Nashville. One day I was in the car with several of the girls while one of the moms drove us around. We drove past a run-down part of town, and a teammate said, 'My dad calls places like these Niggerville.' Then she looked at me and said, 'Sorry, Jenn.'"

More time was allowed to pass in silence as memory after memory flooded my brain. Again, Sophia broke the silence by asking, "What are you noticing."

"Our practice attire was biker shorts and a sports bra. I was the only one on the team with my body type, and the first day, the coach was like, 'Whoa! Look at Jenn and her ghetto booty!' From then on out, the other girls started talking about my ghetto booty too."

More silence. More buzzing in my hands. More memories in my mind.

"What are you noticing?"

"The owner of the theater where I worked never bothered to learn my name. He'd call everyone else by name. But with me, he'd just snap his fingers and say, 'Hey, Girl.'"

I almost always spent most of these sessions crying and wiping away tears; not only because the process was painful, but because hearing myself rattle off experience after experience made me realize how many racialized events had chipped away at my soul and were affecting my spirit on a daily basis. It was astounding the things that came to my mind—memories and thoughts I had long suppressed to the point of even forgetting that they had ever happened.

I was relieved when Sophia would tell me to go to my safe, calm place. It was always a specific place I've traveled to, usually outside of the States, but it was never the same place twice. While international travel is stressful for many, I have the privilege of feeling emotionally safe and calm when I am outside of my national borders, particularly in Latin America. My trips abroad afforded me the ability to blend in with the crowd in some communities. It's a freedom that I relish, crave, and wish every one of my Black brothers and sisters could experience when their spirits are bogged down by being Black in the U.S.

"There's a theme to all of the things you're walking me through."

I looked at her, exhausted and exasperated, knowing I didn't have the answer. "I'm supposed to recognize the theme, aren't I?"

Sophia smiled and nodded. I searched my mind, trying to think about all of the different things that I had brought up over the last few weeks. I had no idea. I was at a loss. Sophia thumbed through her notes, picking a few quotes to read aloud.

"No one else said anything."

"I was the only one who heard it."

"No one else seemed surprised."

"I was the only one shocked by that."

"I looked around to see if anyone else thought that was messed up."

"There were no other Black people there."

She paused. "In all of these traumatic memories, you felt alienated. And now it makes so much sense that you're so big on inclusion and making sure you don't make anyone else feel like they are the only one. Ever."

I honestly hadn't seen the pattern, but as she read those quotes and said those things, it all came so clearly into view. In so many situations, I had been the only one. And since being the only one made me feel unsafe, for my own preservation, I stayed quiet rather than risk retaliation or further emotional pain by standing up for myself. The memories that had surfaced were ones that I had locked away, and often had told no one else about. I was embarrassed by what I had experienced and ashamed because I did nothing in the face of the racism I encountered.

Now brought to light, Sophia provided a safe space for me to talk about my experiences. As an adult, I was able to say all of the things the damaged girl inside of me was too afraid to say when it happened. I was no longer without the language to describe what was happening to me and why it was wrong; I was empowered to stand up against it. Slowly, by giving a voice to these hurts, the grasp these memories had on me grew weaker and weaker. They were no longer my painful, secret memories. These experiences no longer haunted me or made me cower.

As I worked through past hurts, I was also able to address more recent hurts and make progress in the way I related to Ryan's family. I finally arrived at a place where I was no longer afraid to speak freely and with confidence in the face of words and actions I found offensive. I took actions that I felt were necessary, and the best part was that Ryan was at a place in his journey where he understood and stood by me without hesitation.

"I can't in good faith send your relatives our Christmas card this year."

Ryan furrowed his eyebrows in confusion. "OK. Why is that?"

"All summer long your family was egregious. I'm not giving them this photo card. They don't get to gaze upon our Black children while at the same time mocking the death of Black bodies. They don't get to hang this card on their fridge as their ticket to claim they aren't racist."

"I can't argue with that," he said.

And that was that. I used to send the cards because that's the thing you do. But now I wasn't playing that game. Some people may call it petty, but I call it living out my principles. I was done doing things just because I had done them in the past. And Ryan was done asking me to do things to keep the peace at the expense of my own emotional well-being.

"I'm ready to be that guy," Ryan continued. "I'm ready to stand up and speak out against all the crap my family does."

I smiled at him. Ryan had made this promise to me before without knowing what it entailed. I hoped he was ready to make good on what he was saying, but the victory was that my mental health no longer depended on his ability to do so. "I know, babe. And I think you *should* be the one to say something. But the amazing thing is that I don't *need* you to be that guy anymore. I am at a place where I can stand up for myself."

As 2020 came to a close, Sophia and I sat in her office.

"What are three things you've learned about yourself this year?"

I thought about it for a minute. "I am stronger than I think I am. I am capable of creating change. My voice is needed."

Then she asked, "What are three things you've learned about your marriage?"

"Wait," I said, alarmed. "What is this? Are you firing me?"

She gave an airy laugh. "No, I'm not firing you. What are three things you've learned about your marriage?"

"There are still things to discover about Ryan. We actually have a great marriage. And we can survive hard things."

She didn't say anything. I didn't say anything. We sat looking at each other for a few seconds, then I broke eye contact and looked all around the room as I searched my thoughts.

I looked back at her. "I feel really good about things. I mean, what do we talk about now? Where do we go from here?"

"Well, that's the question. You've reached your therapeutic goals."

My eyes started welling up with tears. "Oh my gosh. You *are* firing me."

She laughed again. "I'm not firing you. We have a couple of options. We can come up with a new treatment plan or you can be discharged."

"Discharged? Meaning we won't see each other anymore?"

She nodded.

I sat for a moment as tears fell and then, "My gut is telling me our journey is done."

She nodded again. "Yeah."

Sophia and I scheduled what would be our final session together. One last wrap-up session where I was able to express my gratitude to her and she was able to give me parting words of encouragement. And while I am all for documenting everything to the best of my ability, I prefer to keep those final words between the two of us just for me.

I walked out of her office without looking back. And just like that, my year with Sophia came to a close.

It takes more than love to heal our broken parts

Ryan sometimes jokes that if more people just had quality friendships, he would be out of a job. And it's true! Plenty of people go to therapists because they don't have confidants in their lives. They don't have those amazing, life-giving friendships that allow them to be themselves and also serve as grounded sounding boards for different issues life throws their way.

But sometimes there are hurts that can't be healed through even the most loving of friendships. There is a stigma in seeking out the help of a professional counselor that needs to be overcome. Mental health is just as important as physical health. Instead of being embarrassed, let us be grateful that our community has people specifically trained to help us overcome those things that keep us from leading a full and satisfying life.

Even though my time with Sophia came to an end, I didn't cease to hurt or finish working on myself. The absence of hurt is not the metric of success. There will always be experiences, phrases, visuals that threaten to take me back to the hurt person I was. But I had a reached a place where I had the tools to healthfully cope with negative experiences that would have previously paralyzed me. I can advocate for myself to leave harmful situations and I now have the words to explain to those I love why I am having a certain reaction, rather than letting that reaction sabotage a relationship. I can now talk about my experiences without feeling shame. I am not the same person who first walked into Sophia's office that cold day in January. The year transformed me, and the stakes are too high for me to ever go back to being that person again.

While I love this country I live in, it is not without its faults. I know that many of my Black and brown brothers and sisters experience trauma by virtue of being a person of color living in a country founded on and advanced through principles of white supremacy and superiority. Sadly, too many communities of color do not receive the mental health services that are needed.

My brothers and sisters of color, do not buy into the hype that mental health services are not for you. They are. Take the time you deserve to get the help you need. Don't downplay the hurts you experience in your life. Don't let anyone tell you there is something wrong with you for seeking out professional help. You are worth healing, and that healing not only changes your life, but has the power to transform the generations that come after you. Your family is worth healing. And if you're a person of color who is thinking about going into the counseling profession, I urge you to seriously look into it. Our communities need more counselors of color who understand our collectively shared experiences. Representation matters.

Counseling is not a weakness. It is a legitimate vehicle to wellness.

Chapter 21

It Takes More Than Love To Make An Impact

The journeys of reckoning with race that Ryan and I have taken, while not identical, were interwoven as we learned from one another and even, at times, depended on each other to move forward in our own personal growth. While our journeys aren't done, our mutual dedication to our individual journeys has healed parts of our hearts (both the long-hidden and newly uncovered hurts) in powerful ways.

During one of our check-ins, toward the end of 2020, we paused to reflect on how things have changed for us as individuals and as a couple.

"Ryan, this year was really hard. Like really, really hard."

"Yes, it was," he agreed. "But look where it got us."

"I know. It was awful sometimes, but I wouldn't take it back for anything in the world."

"Me neither. We are different people because of it. Our marriage is stronger because of it."

It was emotional, difficult, and far from fun; but it was necessary. Prior to engaging in the work of really understanding how race was affecting us, there were times when I was convinced that I would be in a marriage where my partner would never be able to empathize with a big part of my existence. Some days, I told myself this was something I would be able to live with. Other days, it made me really sad. These days, I'm grateful that's not the case.

To this day, Ryan and the kids continue to go up to North Dakota without me. Knowing the answer before the question leaves their lips, they always ask if I'm going to accompany them. I know they want their mom to come with them, but I tell them that they will get to bond with their dad in the place where he grew up while I get a little alone time to re-center myself and relax. It's actually become something that I can look forward to.

I don't need to burden my children with my grievances about their grandparents. If one day down the road they ask me about my experiences with or opinions about their grandparents, I won't lie to them. But for now, they have the right to become acquainted with Ryan's parents on their own account. I feel comfortable with that, knowing they are always in the presence of their dad, in whom I now have complete confidence. It's almost as good as if I were going up there myself. He has committed to putting our kids' needs first—if at any time one of them chooses not to go to Fargo or, while in Fargo, says they want to leave, he will. He won't try to convince them to stay in a place where they don't feel comfortable. He will give them what he struggled all those years to give me—relief without question.

Ryan's protection of me and our entire family has grown. In the fall of 2021, Ryan's mom told him that she would be near Omaha and that she wanted to drop in for a visit. Ryan flat out told her no. He said that she wasn't going to be able to come because she and I have a strained relationship. For weeks, I never knew this exchange even happened. It came up in passing. No longer threatened by her presence around my children, I told Ryan that she was welcome to come, but that I would just take a small weekend trip or enjoy a nice Mommy staycation in a hotel.

"No," Ryan said. "Thanks, but no. She's not kicking you out of your house."

I appreciated that he was putting his foot down on how much he would allow his mom to affect what we did as a family. He told me that he made it clear to her that she had to make things right with me before it would be OK for her to come visit. Feeling the sting of this new boundary, Ryan's mom expressed her desire to have a conversation with me. For Ryan's sake, I agreed.

I didn't want to speak with his mom. The desire to have any sort of loving and meaningful relationship with either of Ryan's parents left me long ago. For years, I felt out of place around his family, only accepted in fragments—any part of me that was unfamiliar or challenged their thinking had to be swept to the side. Existing like that can wear on a person, and I had grown tired of trying to be accepted. Take all of me or have none of me.

Ryan, his mom, and I ended up having a FaceTime conversation. It didn't last too long—maybe thirty minutes. This was the first time I had spoken to her since all of my time in therapy—since all of the work I had done on myself to speak up and not be shocked into silence. Almost immediately, she attempted to place blame on me for the dysfunction in our relationship, saying that I ran away from tough conversations.

This time, I didn't freeze up. In fact, I shut it down. "Nope," I said flatly. "I'm going to stop you right there. You don't get to do that." I spoke with a clarity and boldness that she was unfamiliar with. Her countenance betrayed her, and I could tell I was striking a nerve. I saw her face flush as her neck flared up with red splotches. She didn't know this Jenn. She wasn't acquainted with this woman who didn't easily back down.

I can't say that a whole lot came from the conversation as it pertains to our relationship, but for me it was healing. For so long, I had prioritized pseudo harmony over standing up for myself. Though I had tried to speak up in the past, I didn't push back when my concerns were pushed aside. This time, I felt like I was able to say all of the things that had been bottled up inside of me for the past several years without fear or even anger. I left the conversation feeling peace about having spoken my piece. It felt good. It felt strong.

I have gone through a lot of personal changes these past couple of years since I embarked on the journey of unpacking the negative effects that racism has had on me and the relationships I have with those I love, primarily my husband. While Ryan has been on his own journey, we committed to stay on our journey of marriage together. In the summer of 2023, we took our kids back to the place where he and I began—Buenos Aires. We lived there for seven weeks, showed the kids the people and places that are dear to our hearts, and renewed our vows in the church that brought us together.

While my journey of healing from racial trauma started out of a need for relief, it soon morphed into a journey of equipping myself to fortify my own kids against the same traumas. When my work of confronting past hurts took me into parts of my heart and memories that were long deemed off-limits, I felt compelled to keep going because I knew that they, too, would benefit from my working on myself. It's one thing for me to tell them to stand up for themselves. It's another thing for them to see me do it. If I can lead by example while affirming their young voices, they may have a chance at not suffering the pain that feeling voiceless can inflict on one's heart.

I could never have anticipated that while I was taking my journey, the rest of the world would be called upon to reckon with the sins of racism. Once George Floyd was murdered, I realized how much bigger this journey was than myself. On a daily basis, I reminded myself that my kids were going to get older and study American history in school one day. It was inevitable that they were going to read about 2020 in their textbooks and ask me what I did—what part did I play? I'm going to have a lot to share, and I'll say that I did it all for them.

I'm going to tell them how I spoke up about the racism that existed in their extended family.

I'm going to tell them that I fought for all kids to feel like an integral and valued part of their schools.

I'm going to tell them that I fought for everyone to feel seen and heard within their church community.

I'm going to tell them that I told my story in hopes of motivating those who shared my struggles to stand up and tell their stories as well.

I'm going to tell them that I worked to cultivate in them the ability to move fluidly among diverse peoples, offer to use their voices on behalf of others when they felt silenced, and understand the dynamic that race can add to a situation. My hope was to prevent them from having to unlearn many of the things I've watched adults unlearn.

I'm going to tell them these things so that they know that an ordinary person can and should be an agent of change within their sphere of influence when something in the world is awry.

I implore each of you reading this memoir to mobilize and make great strides in achieving equity in our society for all communities. While much of the discussion about anti-oppression in 2020 was focused on Black lives, the movement can and does benefit all communities that are marginalized. If we can evoke and promote compassion for one community, it gets us closer to being able to do that for all communities. It's not about changing the oppressor; it's about eradicating the oppression. Period.

That's why we all have to be in this together. Please, let's make major progress on this. Will your heart be able to take it if we have to watch our kids continue fighting these battles? I know mine won't. I desperately want to free our children up to tackle other national and global problems. Let's release our babies from this burden so that they may use their creativity and ingenuity to solve those other very important pending issues. That can be one of our major gifts to our children.

As I wrote down the lessons I was learning, I found that they applied not only to marriage, but also to friendship, parenthood, professional relationships, and just about any situation in which I was working with another human being. At the end of the day, that's what this is about. It's about showing up as fully human and giving other people the respect that allows them to do the same. It's about learning from the people around us by hearing each other's stories and caring about who they are and what they've been through.

We all want to be seen, heard, accepted, understood, and loved. Every person is deserving of that. Unfortunately, love often gets downgraded to simply being a feeling or an ideal; it becomes so abstract that we don't even know what to reach for.

Love conquers all. All you need is love. Love will find a way. Phrases like these get thrown around so flippantly that they lose their power. Should love be at the root of everything we do? Yes, but we need love *and* action.

Love is Jewel putting her own discomfort aside to call me and properly apologize for hurting me so that I knew she was committed to standing by my side.

Love is Ryan committing himself to therapy because I asked him to do work in his own life that he hadn't even identified yet.

Love is my friend Jessica urging me not go into a certain bathroom stall because of the racist writings she'd observed on the door. She then confronted the clerk on duty and demanded it get cleaned up.

Love is the teacher who visits their students' homes for no other reason than to learn more about the children and families they work with every day.

Love is taking time to really ask a person how they are doing and being prepared to listen to the truth.

Love is going into the voting booth and thinking about how your vote affects populations different from the one(s) you are a member of.

Love is giving your time or resources to someone else to make something better for them without any concern for what acknowledgment may be given you.

Love, without action, is a dream without a plan. This isn't the time to feel overwhelmed about all of the injustice in the world. This is the time to take an honest and sober look at the people and places we can influence and ask ourselves where there is room for improvement.

What are the hiring practices at my place of employment?

What kind of images are normalized in my workplace, home, place of worship, etc.?

Whose off-colored jokes have I discreetly cringed at, yet have not pushed back on?

What courageous conversations have I been putting off?

When decisions are being made, who doesn't have a seat at the table?

As we take a hard look at our spheres of influence with the goal of fighting inequities, the questions will flow. It's our responsibility to not hide from them, but to give them thoughtful and humble consideration with an honest desire to seek out solutions. It does no good to have a dream without a plan. It does no good to love without action.

And let us not fool ourselves into believing that we are acting when we are really not. My prayerful brothers and sisters, I believe in the power of prayer right along with you; but let us not think that the act of praying is action enough. Yes, God is powerful and can do all things, but God can also empower us to take steps to bring healing and relief to those in our midst in a variety of ways. We need to be prayerful *and* do some heavy lifting.

Together, we can do this. We stand on the shoulders of giants who have gotten us this far on the journey toward building bridges of reconciliation and healing. Now it's ours to take and move forward. Start with love, but don't stop there.

It takes more than love.

If you enjoyed this, please leave a review. This is a great way to help indie authors succeed – thank you!

Acknowledgments

Thank you to Uplit Press for taking my story and making it available to other people.

Greg, thank you for your countless hours of workshopping my chapters with me. Your input undoubtedly bolstered the quality of what I put on the page.

Katie, thank you for the part you played in taking a rough manuscript and making it a more complete story.

Daniel, thank you for sharing the highs and lows of your own publishing journey when it came time for me to start my own. I will always love you so much.

A huge thank you to my writing group. Thank you for reading and re-reading parts of this book; your honesty forced me to dig deep and let the reader feel my feelings. I look forward to one day seeing your work in the world.

Thank you to Ayser Salman. Reading your memoir made me think that maybe, just maybe, I could write my story too. Thank you for your accessibility and your advice.

Thank you to my initial readers. You lent me your time in reading what I wrote and sharing your thoughts on what worked and what didn't.

Thank you to my parents. There are not enough words in the English lexicon to express the gratitude I have for you. Your endless support has no boundaries, and I have used your bottomless belief in my abilities as a reminder that I am strong enough to put my story out there.

Sophia. Everything would have turned out very differently if it weren't for your guidance and wisdom. In seeking your counsel, I've discovered truths and lessons that I will carry for a lifetime and pass on to my children. Thank you, thank you, thank you.

To my ultimate hype-woman—the one who tells me I can do anything. Girl, you shouldn't prop me up as much as you do, but I'm grateful for every encouraging word.

Thank you to the small circle of friends with whom I shared the news of this project. Thank you for your quiet whispers of encouragement, your sporadic questions asking me how it was going, or your silent support because I just needed you to know this was happening but didn't want you to ask me anything else about it.

Last, but not least, thank you to my husband, Ryan. While this is my story, you are very much part of it, and your vulnerability is on full display for the world to see. Thank you for being a partner that even my wildest imagination couldn't dream up. I'm grateful for your maturity, tranquility, and your unwavering embrace of the fuller version of myself that I have become. I love you, I love you, I love you.

About the Author

Jenna Winters lives with her husband and four children in Omaha, Nebraska. Whenever she has a spare moment, she can be found enjoying a book (she carries one with her everywhere she goes). The only thing she loves more than reading is traveling. She believes that leaving the comfort zone of one's own community is one of the greatest ways to build empathy for other people.

You can connect with her via her IG at @takesmorethanlove.

UpLitPress.co.uk

Publishing books that make you glad to be part of the human race.

Get a free anthology when you join our mailing list

www.ingramcontent.com/pod-product-compliance
Lightning Source LLC
Chambersburg PA
CBHW021431150726
47989CB00001B/206